Twisted Whiskers

SOLVING YOUR
CAT'S BEHAVIOR PROBLEMS

THE CROSSING PRESS
Berkeley | Toronto

D0117278

Text copyright © 1994 by Pam Johnson

All rights reserved. No part of this book may be reproduced in any form, except brief excerpts for the purpose of review, without written permission of the publisher.

The Crossing Press
A division of Ten Speed Press
P.O. Box 7123
Berkeley, California 94707
www.tenspeed.com

Library of Congress Cataloging-in-Publication Data on file with publisher.

ISBN-13: 978-0-89594-710-9
ISBN-10: 0-89594-710-2

Cover photograph by Nancy Lee Andrews
Cover design by Tara M. Eoff
Text design by Yasmine Nadel
Text drawings by Lewis McClellan

First printing, 1994
Printed in the United States of America

8 9 10 11 12—08 07 06 05

For my parents and my sister. I love you.

And for Ethel.
Thank you for helping me see the world
through the eyes of a cat.
I miss you.

table of contents

introduction

To be a feline behavior consultant takes guts. Not because of anything cats might do, but because you inevitably become jokingly referred to as the "kitty shrink." Whenever I'm at a party or with a group of people and someone asks me what I do for a living, I know it won't be long before the word will spread around the room. "You're a feline WHAT?" is usually someone's first response. Then I spend much of the evening explaining that, "No, I don't teach cats to sit, stay, fetch, or roll over, but rather, I work with both cats and owners to solve behavior problems."

These days there are many animal behaviorists available to help owners. When I started learning about cats, though, many people had never considered calling in an animal behaviorist to help solve problems.

I became a cat lover quite by accident when I adopted two homeless kittens. I didn't know much about cats then but it didn't take long for the love affair to bloom. I became fascinated by cats and how intelligent they seemed. Since I had only grown up having dogs I was intrigued by the different ways cats communicate and what they required from humans. I wanted to know everything. After reading as many books as I could get my hands on, I started observing different cats and their owners (my friends were very patient with me). I wanted to learn how problems arise and how they're solved. I also spent countless hours at veterinarians' clinics (they were equally as patient) observing cats and the variety of problems they encounter. I then knew that the true answers couldn't come from anyone other than the cats themselves. I went straight to the source and began to let the cats teach me. By then I had a good background in feline nutrition, grooming, health, and general care, but I wanted to know what goes on behind those beautiful eyes.

One of the first things I learned about cats is that very few people are lukewarm about them. There are those who passionately love cats and feel they're highly intelligent, graceful, sensitive and beautiful creatures. Then there are the people who feel cats are nothing but aloof, untrainable, furniture-destroying, hair-shedding, furball-vomiting snobs. And, if you're daring enough, try getting a group of dog lovers and cat lovers together. All you have to do to set off an evening of heated discussion is ask which makes the better pet, a dog or a cat. Dog owners will argue that cats don't "do" anything. Well, those of us who have spent any amount of time with a cat know just ridiculous that old argument is. Cats just make everything they do look so effortless.

I think that, as owners, we take our intelligent and intriguing cats for granted. Cats make life so convenient for us by being very clean, quiet and graceful. They don't need to be walked, are able to handle long periods alone, and they don't disturb the neighbors with their barking. Because cats do make life so easy for us we sometimes overlook their needs. When a cat behaves in an undesirable way, we all too often assume he's being spiteful, stubborn, or willfully destructive.

This book is to help you figure out what your little companion is trying to communicate. Hopefully you'll find the solutions so you can bridge the distance that's come between the two of you because of the problem. Begin by viewing that furry little feline as your own private teacher. Although he may not speak in words, he's definitely telling you something.

As I'm sure you're already aware, this book is not intended to be a replacement for veterinary care. Always seek your vet's advice first, even if you're sure the problem is behavioral. Your vet may uncover a medical condition that's causing the undesirable behavior. Don't hesitate to contact your vet with questions; he or she is there to help you keep your cat healthy and happy.

In an effort to be fair, I've alternated referring to cats as males and females throughout this book. I don't want to imply favoritism because I do love both male and female cats equally. And, because I feel that a cat is a very important member of the family, you'll never find me referring to any feline as an "it."

Because I'm unable to make a house call to you personally, I hope that within these pages you find the tools you need to be your own feline behavior consultant. You already have the most important qualification of all—your love for your cat.

chapter 1

Understanding Behavior Modification

The secret to living in harmony with a cat is understanding that her so-called undesirable behavior is actually her best way of communicating to you that something's wrong. Since a cat can't sit you down for a heart-to-heart chat about why she's upset, the next best thing is to get your attention. If you give up the notion that your cat's being spiteful and manipulative and start looking at what she's trying to communicate, you stand a very good chance of solving the problem. Very often when I make a house call to do a behavior session it's really to serve as the interpreter between cat and owner. I listen to the owner describe the problem, then I ask lots of questions. I look around to get a good sense of the cat's environment. Finally, I spend time with the cat. After I've had some individual time with the kitty, I ask the owner to come in so I can watch how they relate. All this information allows me to put the pieces of the puzzle together to help the owner solve the *reason* for the behavior problem and use modification techniques to rebuild the bond between them.

We need to be more sensitive to our cats' needs because we ask so much of them in terms of being obedient, loving companions. All too often *we're* the reason our cat may have to suffer through behavior problems. For example: We love how convenient it is that our cat uses a litter box so we never have to run home in time to walk her the way our dog-owning friends do; in return, our responsibility is to keep the litter box clean. When we don't fulfill our responsibility, the cat may start using a different area of the house. Another example: It's a normal behavior in a cat to scratch and visually mark objects with her claws. She's not being destructive—she's just being a cat! Our responsibility is to provide an adequate scratching post. Too often we neglect this and then spend so much time getting mad at the cat for scratching the furniture. With just a little more understanding about what a cat needs and why those needs exist, you can achieve the relationship you've always wanted with her. Although you view your cat as a member of the family, don't humanize her so much that you neglect those feline needs.

Any behavior problem can be the result of an underlying medical condition, so please have your cat checked by the veterinarian first. Don't assume it's a behavior problem until the vet has given your cat an exam. I can't tell you how many times owners have called me to complain about their cat not using the litter box. After insisting they go to the vet before I'll agree to see her, it turns out she has cystitis. There are many other times I've been called about a formerly loving cat turning aggressive. Whenever the owner picks her up she hisses and tries to bite. Many times the vet discovers a painful abscess (usually the result of a cat fight) is the cause of the aggression because it hurts the cat to be touched. So please, don't skip this very important first step. See your vet.

When I do a consultation I try to limit it to one or two sessions (unless it's an aggression problem or other specific situation that requires a slower approach in short intervals). I have two reasons for trying to limit how many sessions I do with one cat. First, I realize that by the time owners contact me, they've probably already spent more money than they planned to (whether on replacing urine-soaked carpets, buying endless brands of litter, scratching posts, numerous vet visits, etc.). The other reason is that I want the owners to implement the behavior modification techniques so they'll become more perceptive to their cat's moods and/or needs. The best way to rebuild the cat/owner bond is to have them do the work together. Phone contact is always encouraged in order to track the owner's progress and provide support.

Behavior modification takes time so don't get discouraged if results don't happen overnight. You're retraining the cat's mind and breaking those old negative thought patterns. For the success to be long-term you have to give your cat time. If you're consistent, patient and positive, it will work.

"Negative" Training

When training a dog, you use her natural desire to please the more dominant "pack leader" (in this case, you). With my dog Annabelle, all I have to do is look at her with a stern expression, and she immediately knows her behavior is unacceptable. With the cat (who isn't a pack animal) this method doesn't work. Your cat won't be affected by that stern expression. And resorting to punishment doesn't work; it will only be perceived as a threat to her safety. If you've been spanking your cat, yelling at her, rubbing her nose in her accidents, exiling her in isolation, or using any other such methods, please stop now. It doesn't work, it never has, it never will. The biggest mistake you make when you hit a cat is that you'll only be training her to be afraid of you. She won't be able to differentiate between the hand coming toward her for petting or for hitting. She'll assume the worst and either cringe, run or become defensive. When you bring a cat over to a spot on the carpet where she had an accident and you rub her nose in it you create a worse situation. She won't associate that with your telling her it's bad to urinate in that spot. Instead, she'll think it's bad to urinate at all. She'll seek other places, or worse, hold it until you're not around. She may also become afraid to use her litter box. Your only hope is to figure out *why* she's doing these things and then reduce her anxiety so she'll respond to the various behavior modification techniques described in this book.

Positive Reinforcement

This is the only way to go. All the techniques you'll read about in the following chapters are based on positive reinforcement. Instead of filling the cat's life with a bunch of "nos," you're going to structure it so she gets what she needs but in the way you prefer. For example: If your cat is scratching on the furniture, provide her with a scratching post she'll want to use. Encourage her to use the post through playtime and praise. If you don't want a cat to do something just give her a better option. Keep that little thought in mind and you won't go wrong. Cats are smart; they'll let you know when you've done it right.

In this book I stress *praise* as an important tool in training. The tone of your voice can have quite an impact on your cat. For instance, during grooming or medicating, a soothing tone throughout the process followed by much praise can make the procedure anywhere from bearable to absolutely enjoyable.

Positive reinforcement can be used in correcting any behavior problem (in combination with modification techniques) from aggression and hyperactivity to depression and lethargy. It works because it helps to relieve the stress a cat inevitably feels during a behavior crisis.

Positive reinforcement:

- reduces stress
- builds self-confidence
- accelerates training success
- strengthens owner/cat bond
- encourages companion cats to get along
- adds more joy in a cat's life

Remote Control Training

This is the only negative form of training I use. The reason I call it remote control is that your cat won't directly connect the correction with you, her loving owner. An example of remote control training is coating electrical wires with pepper sauce or bitter orange so that the cat won't chew on them. Another example is lining empty soda cans (put a few pennies in them and tape over the opening) along the kitchen counter to train the cat not to jump up. She'll soon learn that whenever she jumps up there she knocks over these noisy, scary objects. In time she'll know to avoid those negative places (even after the cans are no longer there), but she won't know you had anything to do with it. Humans are a sneaky bunch.

Remote control training is very useful when it comes to setting boundaries. The trick is to make certain your cat doesn't associate it with you. And always combine it with that good old positive reinforcement whenever she does the right thing.

No cat is going to be perfectly behaved all of the time. People aren't, so how can we expect it from cats?

If you're dealing with a kitten, a cat that's been in a former home, or one that's undergone some form of stress, be patient with her.

chapter 2

Feline Communication

A cat has special marking glands that release a scent so he can properly identify objects within his territory as his own. He'll very often use the facial scent glands to mark his territory by rubbing his chin and cheeks along the object (such as a table leg, chair, doorway, etc.). The marking done by the scent glands on the forehead is also reserved for friendly encounters—such as two familiar cats greeting each other. Outdoors, when two feline friends meet up with one another they sniff nose to nose, turn to do some anal sniffing and include some forehead rubbing. This is all part of a friendly greeting. Your own cat will also rub his forehead on you (sometimes it'll seem like he's almost butting you with his head). This should be viewed as an affectionate greeting. He may also turn and present his hindquarters for anal sniffing. Don't be insulted if he suddenly does this while in your lap or while you're petting him; it's just his version of a friendly handshake. I just pet my cat on the back, then reach over and scratch him on the chin or behind the ears. He turns back around and we continue our petting and forehead rubbing.

Scratching objects, in addition to conditioning the nails and stretching muscles, provides another function. It leaves the object with a visual and an olfactory mark. There are glands between the toes that secrete a scent when a cat scratches. If you don't want your cat to scratch your furniture, you need to provide an acceptable scratching post (discussed in Chapter 7). Many people believe that scratching is for sharpening claws but it isn't. Scratching removes the dead outer layer of the nail to reveal the new growth underneath. When you also consider that scratching helps to stretch out muscles and deposit a comforting scent for the cat you can begin to understand the overpowering need he has to have adequate scratching surfaces.

On the pads of the cat's paws are sweat glands. This is how cats help themselves to keep cool (they also pant to help dispel body heat). If you look at your veterinarian's examination table the next time your cat is being checked over, you'll probably be able to see some moist little paw prints. Intact male cats also have a scent gland at the end of the tail. Very often this gland causes the tail to have a greasy look to it as the sebaceous secretion builds up. This condition is referred to as "stud tail." Perhaps intact toms aren't as fastidious about grooming so they neglect this little area. Neutering eliminates stud tail.

There's another set of scent glands that aren't as subtle as the facial scent glands. This special pair of glands is known as the anal glands. The purpose of these anal glands is to mark the cat's feces with a scent. These glands are supposed to get expressed naturally as the cat's stool passes out of the rectum. Unfortunately, they don't always get emptied and can occasionally become clogged up. To relieve the discomfort the cat may frequently lick his genitals. You may also notice an unpleasant odor coming from your cat's back end. Your veterinarian can take care of the problem by manually expressing the glands. Your cat is less likely to suffer from clogged anal glands if he's fed good quality food with adequate fiber.

When it comes to marking, urine and feces are a cat's most convenient forms. Urine spraying is a form of communication done mainly by males (but some females will also spray). The urine that's sprayed for scent marking is mixed with a viscous fatty material (from a special gland that provides the scent). The smell of tomcat urine is quite unmistakable. Spraying an object is a cat's way of leaving his calling card. He is identifying an object as his own or a part of his territory. The scent tells other cats who was here and how long ago he passed by. In most cases, neutering a male cat will eliminate his desire to spray. In the few cases where it doesn't, behavior modification techniques can then be used to help a neutered cat overcome his need to spray (covered in Chapter 6).

Cats bury their waste so as not to attract predators to their nest. This is one of the many reasons we find cats to be such convenient pets. In the wild, the dominant cat of the area doesn't always bury his feces, preferring to leave them on display along commonly used pathways. He may also leave fecal droppings along the boundaries of his territory in addition to spraying bushes and trees. When it comes to your indoor cat, if he doesn't bury his feces in the litter he's not trying to show dominance over you. As the provider of his food and shelter you're already the established mother cat. Not all cats were given adequate litter training by their mothers, and maybe your little kitty didn't quite get the hang of how to cover.

A Cat's Touch

Cats react to being stroked differently than dogs. Cats very often don't enjoy the constant physical contact that a dog craves. Prolonged contact can become confusing for a cat since they generally don't touch each other very much in the wild. As an owner you may have experienced this "contact confusion" when you're stroking your cat and he suddenly becomes aggressive. Sometimes he gets in such a relaxed state that it momentarily startles him. More on this type of aggression in Chapter 8.

A cat uses his paws for initial investigation purposes. The paws are also formidable weapons. A warning swipe will not involve claws. It's just that—a warning. If you don't pay attention to the warning, the next one or two swipes will be harder and may include a little bit of the claws. If the cat is pushed to full-fledged anger, the paw swipe will involve fully bared claws.

A cat's touch can be so gentle that it hardly even qualifies as a touch. Sometimes when I open my eyes in the morning I'll find my cat, Olive, watching me. She'll then reach out with one paw and ever-so-gently touch my cheek—I'll barely feel it. She has never done it with a claw exposed. It's her very gentle way of saying, "Good morning."

Oh, Those Eyes, Those Lips...

Many people mistakenly believe that a cat can see in total darkness. This simply is not true. Cats do see when it's so dark that to our human eyes it appears to be totally black. The cat has a reflective layer at the back of the eye called the tapetum lucidum. This layer acts as a mirror, reflecting light back into the retina. This allows the cat to use every bit of available light. The *tapetum lucidum* is what causes the cat's eyes to glow in some flash pictures.

A cat's eyes are large for the size of his head. Perhaps those big eyes are one of the reasons we find cats so fascinating. I love to watch a cat's eyes as he watches the birds outside the window with great intensity, or as he slowly blinks in relaxation while resting in a favorite spot.

A cat has a third eyelid known as the nictitating membrane. The eyelid acts as a protective layer as he travels through tall grass or bushy areas. When not in use, the eyelid rests in the inner corner of the eye. When needed, it slides upward. You can sometimes see the third eyelid on a sleeping cat when his eyes are partially open. It will almost look as if his eyes have rolled back into his head, but it's actually the third eyelid you're seeing. The third eyelid can also be visible during eye infections, injuries, disease, or if a foreign body gets lodged in the eye. If your cat's third eyelid remains exposed, consider it a warning that something's wrong and have him checked by the veterinarian.

Does a cat see in color? Research indicates that a cat does have the ability to distinguish between some colors but not nearly as many as we can. But when you think about it, why would an animal who hunts mostly at dawn and at night need to see colors? *Movement* is what a cat needs to see and his eyes are certainly well equipped for that. He has excellent peripheral vision and an incredible ability to concentrate on his target.

The whiskers help a cat to judge if an opening will accommodate his body (unless you've overindulged him when it comes to between-meal snacks and his width far exceeds the whiskers' length). The whiskers also help a cat navigate around objects in the dark by sensing changes in air currents. There are four rows of whiskers on either side of the muzzle. At the root of each one are lots of sensitive nerve endings. The top two rows move independently of the lower two. The position of your cat's whiskers can also give you an indication of what's going on in his mind. For instance, whiskers spread out and forward indicate that he's alert and ready for action. If the whiskers are facing more to the sides and spread out then he's probably in a relaxed mood. If the whiskers are flattened against his cheeks, then he's probably afraid of something.

Good hearing is vital for an animal who hunts for a living. Cats hear much better than humans do. Cats turn their ears to catch the smallest of sounds to allow it to funnel down the pinnae (the cone-shaped part of the ear). You've probably experienced firsthand how incredible your cat's hearing is as he comes running from the farthest end of the house when you so much as touch the can opener or open a bag of dry food. In terms of body language, forward-facing ears indicate relaxation, confidence, investigation, or a friendly greeting. A cat who knows you and doesn't view you as a threat will hold his ears forward in order to be receptive to whatever sound you might make. During aggressive states ears are in the down position. For battle, they're flattened against the head to reduce the chance of being injured by an opponent's teeth or claws.

Inside the cat's mouth is a very interesting organ called the Jacobson's organ (or vomeronasal organ). The opening of the Jacobson's organ is on the upper palate behind the front teeth and is used for analyzing scents that the cat considers interesting (for instance, a male will use the Jacobson's organ when he comes across a female scent). When the organ is in use the cat will appear to be grimacing with his mouth half open. This is called a *flehmen* reaction (a German word with no English translation). The cat captures the scent on his tongue, curling it in order to lift the scent up to the Jacobson's organ. Even though this is done mostly by males in response to a female scent, all cats use the Jacobson's organ at one time or another when they come across an interesting scent that requires closer investigation.

The cat's tongue, with its backward-facing barbs, helps to remove loose hairs, debris and parasites from the coat. In the wild, the barbs help rasp meat from the bones of captured prey. The roughness of the tongue is also used by a mother cat to stimulate her newborn kittens to get their respiratory systems up and running. Because of the direction the barbs face, cats are unable to get rid of all the hair they collect during grooming so it ends up having to be swallowed. This can result in dreaded hairballs. If your cat swallows too much hair he may have trouble passing it through his system. The hairball may find its way back up by being vomited out of the stomach, or it may go all the way through the intestines and get passed in the feces. If your cat vomits hairballs or if you can see a lot of hair in the feces, speak to your vet about using a hairball remedy. This is a malt-flavored gel that comes in a tube. It's basically just a very mild laxative to lubricate the system and help the hairball to pass. Adding adequate fiber to the diet can help as well (refer to Chapter 5 for information on fiber). Regular brushing will greatly reduce the amount of hair your cat ingests. Stressed and bored cats tend to do an excessive amount of grooming so be aware of potential hairball problems. If the situation isn't controlled, hairballs can cause a blockage in the intestines.

The Voice

What a vocabulary! From a friendly greeting to a loud protest to a scream of terror, cats have quite a lot to say to us. As an owner you quickly learn your cat's language and can differentiate between the "I want to go out" meow from the "My litter box is too dirty" meow. Some cats are more talkative than others (such as the very chatty Siamese). Olive does a running commentary on just about everything I do at home.

The meow of acknowledgment (sounds impressive, doesn't it?) is that little noise your cat makes when you say his name or when he sees you walk in the room.

The request meow is the feline version of "please." You may hear this as he stands by the door, waiting to go out. You might also hear several request meows when you're in the kitchen and he thinks it's even remotely close to mealtime.

The complaint meow is that "I'm not really too pleased with this situation" sound that your cat makes when his patience is starting to wear thin. This may occur during grooming, if he's restrained for any reason, or if you won't let him get to something he really wants.

The chirp is a sound an excited cat makes when observing prey. You've probably heard your cat chirping and chattering as he watches birds outside the window. This is usually accompanied by a flicking and twitching tail motion.

Hissing is a cat's powerful audible warning system. He opens his mouth and releases a force of air. It lets us know we've overstepped our bounds and are to back off. Spitting is sometimes done in conjunction with hissing. Spitting is an involuntary reaction that occurs when a cat is startled, much the same way we might gasp when frightened by something suddenly.

Growling is a more serious warning that a cat will use as a "distance-increasing" behavior. A growl means to seriously back off. A kitten or cat may also growl when he snatches a choice piece of food for himself and goes off to a hiding place to devour his "catch" in private.

The mating cry is something we've all heard at one time or another. The lonely sound of a tom crying in the yard of a female in estrus has inspired many an owner to toss a shoe or pan of water in his direction.

Howling is something some older cats do when they feel they're alone in the house or if they become disoriented (especially if their hearing has become impaired). Usually, calling out to your cat, or in the case of hearing-impaired cats, letting him see you will stop the howling.

There are many other variations on meow that your cat makes, and as you listen more closely to him you'll begin to distinguish their meanings. Part of the pleasure of living with a cat is learning his language.

The Mystery of the Purr

The cat's purr has always been somewhat of a mystery. Nobody has ever been able to positively identify exactly where it comes from. There are a few theories, such as the vibrations of the false vocal cords or blood turbulence in the chest. We do know that cats purr during both inhalation and exhalation, stopping only to swallow. I love it that the purr remains a mystery.

In the beginning, the purr starts as a way for the kittens and mother to communicate. The mother probably purrs to help kittens locate her (from the vibrations of the purr) and to comfort them. Kittens purr as they nurse (perhaps to let mama know that all's well). We associate purring with a contented cat but that's not always the case. Cats will sometimes purr when backed in a corner by an attacker. Some experts believe it's either to calm themselves or the attacker. Cats have also been known to purr when terminally ill. That may also be to help calm themselves.

In your cat's day-to-day life, the purr takes on different meanings. You may notice that he purrs as he waits in anticipation as you prepare his dinner. He may also purr when soliciting some affection or attention from you. We humans have always been suckers for a cat's purr. There's nothing quite as reassuring as listening to your cat purr while sitting in your lap, to let you know there's no place else he'd rather be than with you.

Body Language

Cats don't wag their tails the way dogs do. A lashing back and forth of the cat's tail indicates agitation. As that agitation turns to anger, the lashing grows more intense. What starts as a flicking of the tail in annoyance can end up being a sweepingly rapid lashing done by one very perturbed feline.

An upright tail is used in friendly greeting or if the cat is actively moving within an area in which he feels confident. When two feline friends meet their tails will be up and they'll engage in a round of nose-to-nose sniffing, followed by anal sniffing. A cat who flicks the tip of his upright tail at you is giving you a friendly greeting.

The tail in a down position can indicate relaxation, but an arched tail in the down position indicates an aggressive posture.

A cat who feels threatened may assume a defensive posture by turning sideways and puffing out the hairs along his back and tail, with his whiskers flattened against the sides of his cheeks. This is the Halloween cat image we're all familiar with. Hopefully, this posture will intimidate the attacker enough so he'll go on his way. An offensive posture involves a direct stare, whiskers facing forward, pupils constricted, body squarely facing the intended target. For more on the various types of aggressive behaviors, refer to Chapter 8.

Cats love to play and they solicit playtime in many ways. Your cat may dart around you, chasing imaginary prey, or he may make playful swipes at something you're using (such as a pen). When that doesn't work he may roll over on his side right in front of you (as Olive is doing to me right this very minute) with a devilish look in his eyes.

chapter 3

Healing the Mind

An Introduction to the Bach Flower Remedies

For those of you familiar with the Bach Flower Remedies and their application in behavior modification, this chapter will come as no big news. For those of you unfamiliar with holistic medicine, this chapter may cause you to raise an eyebrow and perhaps begin to doubt my credibility. My hope, though, is that your introduction to the Bach Flower Remedies will provide you with an added avenue toward solving behavior problems.

All the behavior modification techniques recommended in this book stand alone as effective and complete methods without the use of any added holistic preparations. I've included the Bach Flower Remedies as something I've found to be a successful boost to retraining. In my years working with feline behavior, I've always tried to keep track of the progress and value that *certain* drugs/treatments/therapies have on behavior modification. On the traditional side, there are drugs like antianxiety tranquilizers and progestins to assist in stopping undesirable behavior.

While in many cases these drugs do actually succeed, there can be side effects (some very serious), and since drug therapy can't be done long-term, the behavior can resurface when the drug therapy ends. While I find drugs like valium to be a very necessary tool in certain behavior disorders, I prefer, whenever possible, to keep things natural and to work on bringing the cat back into balance. I will never recommend that an owner ask the veterinarian to put a cat on valium unless specific behavior modification techniques are followed so the cat can be weaned off the tranquilizer while retaining the positive behavior changes. And, as far as progestins go, I feel the side effects associated with them are too risky for our beloved companions. If your veterinarian recommends drug therapy for any behavior problem, be sure he or she has made you completely aware of all potential risks and side effects. Follow all instructions concerning the dosage, administration, and withdrawal (some drugs require a gradual weaning off by reduction rather than abruptly ceasing the medication).

When it comes to physical or behavioral problems, I've received a lot of assistance from the many forms of holistic medicine. Even though I've had success with methods such as herbal therapy, I'm not including them in this book. Even natural medicines can have side effects and require precise diagnosis and preparation. Not all herbs are harmless. I would not recommend that you attempt to include them as therapy for your cat unless you're familiar with herbal medicine or can seek counsel from a holistic practitioner. There is one form of holistic therapy that I use regularly in my behavior sessions and recommend to everyone. This therapy remarkably addresses the emotional and psychological aspects of behavior problems without any side effects or risks.

The Bach Flower Remedies were discovered by a well-respected English homeopathic physician and bacteriologist, Dr. Edward Bach, in the 1930s. Dr. Bach observed the mood swings that accompanied the physical ills of his patients. He believed these mood swings were part of the physical illness and that treating the emotional side was an important aspect of treating the disease. He recognized that a negative state of mind affected the body's energy and that anxiety, fear, worry, etc., left the body vulnerable. Dr. Bach realized the connection between body, mind and soul and the importance of all of them in healing. Disease, he believed, was due to the body, mind and soul not being in harmony.

Dr. Bach developed thirty-eight remedies made from the essences of specific flowers. They are harmless, dilute, totally natural and have no side effects whatsoever. Unlike drugs or some herbal medications, if you take the wrong remedy, nothing will happen—literally nothing.

As most everyone knows, plants have been used for medicinal healing for ages. Dr. Bach distinguished between physical symptom-relieving plants and those that had the power to heal on a higher level.

The Bach Flower Remedies work not by attacking a particular disease but on a deeper level by filling the body with the virtue that the higher self needs. Dr. Bach felt that was the pathway to peace. He compared it to the inspiration felt from listening to beautiful music. They are so natural and safe that they're compatible with any other medical treatment. No overdosing can occur. Because this form of therapy is so totally harmless, they're a wonderful alternative for untrained people, whereas other natural treatments require familiarity with possible side effects, accurate preparation and knowledge of compatibility with other treatments. All that's required to use the Bach Flowers is to be perceptive and sensitive to the patient you wish to help.

Most health food stores carry these remedies. There are also several books available if you're interested in learning more about the history of the remedies and becoming familiar with the qualities of each one. When buying the remedies, start off by getting just the few you'll need at the time. If different emotional situations arise in the future that require additional remedies, you can then enlarge your own collection over time. For multicat owners, you may especially want to familiarize yourself with all 38 remedies.

A note of caution: There are other brands of "flower essences" available but only the ones labeled BACH are the original. You may come across brands that claim to be equal to or the same as the original Bach Remedies, but in my experience only the Bach Flower Remedies have worked successfully.

Diagnosing

To correctly diagnose which remedy will be appropriate for your cat you must put aside *your* feelings and try to accurately interpret *her* emotions. For example: You may be furious with her because of her recent aggression and are so sure the behavior is spiteful and mean. Put aside your feeling and try to put yourself in her place. You might then discover that it's actually *fear* that's causing the aggression. By looking at the world through her eyes, you stand a very good chance of pinpointing the source of her fear.

Always keep love in your heart when diagnosing. You are not just prescribing an antibiotic for an intestinal disorder. You're trying to understand the emotions of an animal who is unable to speak for herself.

As behavior is corrected and your cat's body-mind-spirit seem in harmony again, you can stop the particular remedy. At another time in life, she may need it again or another combination if a situation arises.

Preparation

- Into a one-ounce glass dropper bottle put 2 drops of each selected remedy. Limit the number of Bach Flower Remedies to four if possible, to enable them to work most effectively together.
- Fill the bottle three quarters full with spring water (non-carbonated). Don't use distilled water (it's essentially "dead" water). Never use tap water.
- Replace the cap and shake vigorously many times (at least one hundred times).
- Label your treatment bottle so you'll remember which remedies you used. Store in the refrigerator for up to two weeks.

Note: Your original concentrated stock bottles will keep indefinitely if stored away from light. The original concentrated stock bottle contains brandy as a preservative. But, unless you're opposed to the use of alcohol in any form at all, you need not worry about it harming your cat. The amount of brandy in the number of drops of however many remedies selected for treatment is of a minute quantity. Also remember you're diluting it even further when you add the drops to the spring water. As long as you're sure to use spring water (because it remains fresher longer) and never tap water (it goes stale quickly), you won't need to add any brandy as a preservative to your treatment bottle. Store your treatment bottle in the refrigerator and it will last two weeks. If you live in a warm climate and are unable to keep the treatment bottle refrigerated then you'll need to add a teaspoon of brandy as a preservative. If you'd rather not use alcohol, cider vinegar can be substituted instead.

Dosage

- Give 4 drops four times a day until behavior changes (this can range anywhere from a few days to several weeks).

If you can drop the 4 drops directly on the tongue easily, without causing *any* stress to the cat, that's the fastest way to administer. If not, just add the drops to a little food or in the drinking water. I sometimes add it to a teaspoon of yogurt which most cats will view as a treat. Don't contaminate the dropper by allowing it to come in contact with the cat's tongue or any food.

To start you off on becoming familiar with the Bach Flowers, I've listed some of the remedies I frequently use in animal behavior counseling.

Negative State	Suggested Remedies
Anxiety attacks, fear for no apparent reason. Good for hypersensitive cats.	Aspen
Intolerant, overreacts to small things. Unable to see the good in others. Beech is helpful for the cat with an inner rigidity, not allowing a new cat, dog or baby into her life. It will help her become more accepting and less critical of the differences in her new companion.	Beech
Passive, subservient, individually not well developed.	Centaury
Possessive, domineering, needs to be the center of attention. Gets angry if she doesn't get her own way. Use this remedy during second pet introductions if your resident cat seems possessive of you.	Chicory
Seems absent-minded. Lacks interest in the present. Confused, lack of vitality.	Clematis
Compulsive self-groomer, chronic constipation, poor self-image during physical ailments (such as wounds, skin allergies, etc.). This remedy is most often used for cleansing. Good for obese cats.	Crab Apple
Discouragement, despondency, depression due to a setback (such as during illness).	Gentian
Despair, complete hopelessness, not wanting to try again but will if pushed. Expects failure (more severe than Gentian).	Gorse
Jealousy, hatred, actively aggressive, anger, rage, easily hurt feelings. In need of feeling loved. This remedy can be used when introducing a second cat if your resident cat displays absolute rage and anger toward the newcomer.	Holly

Negative State	Suggested Remedies
For bereavement. Wants to stay in past memories, doesn't see the happiness in the present. Homesick.	Honeysuckle
Obesity, sedentary living, trouble getting back into life after illness. Mental fatigue.	Hornbeam
Impatient, little tolerance, irritable, restless, jumpy. This remedy can help encourage your cat's tolerance when introducing a second cat.	Impatience
Full of doubt, inferiority complex. Reluctance to try things because of certainty of failure. This remedy is an excellent one to try when you're retraining a cat to a litter box again, especially if she has a negative association with the box (perhaps from a bout with cystitis).	Larch
Fear of being alone, fear of known things (such as people, dogs, fireworks, thunder, etc.), timidity, shyness.	Mimulus
Appears gloomy for no apparent reason (the moodiness may come and go in a cycle), passive, introverted.	Mustard
Physical/mental fatigue, exhaustion following a long physical illness.	Olive
Acute sense of panic, sheer terror, body rigid with fear.	Rock Rose
Mood fluctuations, erratic. May alternate between hunger and loss of appetite or tenderness and anger.	Scleranthus

Negative State	Suggested Remedies
Unhappy. Sorrow following a traumatic event (such as an accident, death of a family member). Needs comfort but unable to accept comforting. Shock. This remedy is also good for aggression stemming from a physical or emotional shock.	Star of Bethlehem
Mental anguish and complete despair to where no light is seen at the end of the tunnel. Absolutely no joy in life (more severe than Gentian and Gorse).	Sweet Chestnut
High-strung, keyed up, too enthusiastic, unable to relax.	Vervain
Dominating, aggressive, tyrannical. A bully.	Vine
Holds on to old patterns. Slow adjustment to new things (such as a new home, new family member). Sensitivity to disruptions. Walnut can be helpful during retraining to a litter box. Also, it's an excellent remedy if you're unable to touch or brush your cat without an aggressive episode due to past negative association. Walnut is wonderful during transitions to help balance emotions.	Walnut
Withdraws from involvement with family, isolated, detached, prefers to keep to herself. Good for cats who tend to hide during illness.	Water Violet
Chronic illness. Completely passive, no spark. Always seems bored, surrenders to life's struggles and challenges and no longer responds to any interaction from you.	Wild Rose
Self-pity, seems resentful over hardships in life. Sulky, turns negativity inward to create a chip on her shoulder.	Willow

I've only listed 26 of the remedies I tend to use most. By learning more about all the remedies you'll be able to match them perfectly to your cat's current negative state.

There is one more remedy I'd like to introduce: the Rescue Remedy, which is the most well known of all the 38. It's the only one that's a mixture of other remedies and is used for shock (emotional or physical). Rescue Remedy consists of Cherry Plum, Star of Bethlehem, Impatiens, Rock Rose and Clematis. Rescue Remedy is made up to be twice the strength of the other remedies. You add 4 drops from the stock bottle into a one-ounce dropper bottle with spring water. The dosage will vary depending on the emergency. You can either add 4 drops from the treatment bottle to food or water at least four times a day, or in acute cases (such as an injured or unconscious animal), you can use the Rescue Remedy to moisten lips or gums every twenty minutes as needed. When there's no water available, a couple of drops straight from the concentrated stock bottle can be used. I carry one bottle of the Rescue Remedy in my purse (in addition to a bottle kept at home) just for emergencies.

Consulting a Bach handbook will provide you with more specific instructions. The Rescue Remedy isn't a replacement for emergency medical care but rather an assist while on the way to the vet or while waiting for help to arrive.

The Rescue Remedy can also be used after routine surgeries (such as spaying or neutering), especially if your cat is very fearful of the veterinary hospital. Another surgery that may be helped tremendously by the Rescue Remedy in terms of emotional healing is declawing, although I sincerely hope you won't feel the need to have your cat declawed (refer to Chapter 7 on scratching behavior). If the surgery has already been done, the Rescue Remedy may help her adjust. In addition, the Rescue Remedy can be used during serious illness.

During aggressive episodes you can spike your cat's water with the Rescue Remedy to help during the crisis. (You must find the cause of the aggression, though; refer to Chapter 8.)

Rescue Remedy can be a valuable tool during introduction of a second pet if tempers start flaring. In a crisis, it can be mixed in the food or water and can also be used straight from the stock bottle. Both resident cat and newcomer will benefit.

If after reading this chapter you're still very skeptical about the value of Bach flower therapy, I urge you to learn more about it. The Bach Flower Remedies have been used for years by holistic professionals, doctors, dentists, veterinarians and animal behaviorists. If you're concerned about them just having a placebo effect, I strongly suggest you read *Bach Flower Remedies to the Rescue*, by Gregory

Vlamis (Healing Arts Press). The book contains testimonials from respected veterinarians about the successful treatment of animals. After all, animals don't know what's being administered so they can't have a preconceived idea of its success or failure the way humans tend to.

For a list of more recommended reading on Bach Flower therapy, refer to the Suggested Reading List in the back of this book.

chapter 4

Play Therapy

What is Play Therapy? It's how I set up specific games with specific toys for each individual cat's problem. When your cat was a kitten, playtime came quite naturally and he was often able to amuse himself with anything from a crumpled piece of paper accidentally tossed on the floor to the dangling laces on a pair of running shoes by the back door. Over the years, though, some cats lose their desire/ability to play or they get too overwhelmed by negative conditions within the home. Obese cats get caught up in a cycle of eating and sleeping, maybe even eventually reaching a point where the extra weight makes movement too uncomfortable. Combined with the proper reducing diet, Play Therapy can help a flabby feline lose the weight, improve his circulation and add years to his life. For aggressive cats, Play Therapy can help release the negative energy in a positive way, allowing the cat to begin viewing his surroundings as less threatening. Nervous cats need the distraction of Play Therapy to ease stress. Depressed cats will build self-confidence and find that forgotten spark for life again. Play Therapy eliminates boredom, increases health, and reduces stress. Because this form of play involves the use of "interactive" toys (meaning you and your cat play together), the bond between you grows and strengthens. For owners with nervous, aggressive or bored cats, rebuilding that emotional bond is needed because there has probably been some distance between the two of you due to behavior problems.

The interactive toys I'm going to recommend will serve some very important functions. First, because they require you to handle them, they allow you to control the pace of play and can vary their function based on your cat's need (to ease aggression, calm anxiety, etc.). Because your involvement is required it does wonders for strengthening the bond between the two of you. In households, using an interactive toy can help two cats get along better. And for those owners who say their cats have refused to play in the past, interactive toys and the correct play method will wake up the sleeping kitten in even the most sedentary cat.

Interactive Toys

The Kitty Tease, made by the Galkie Company, has been my absolute favorite for years. Many similar toys have come along since its appearance but as far as I'm concerned, you can't beat this great original for durability, effectiveness and simplicity. It basically looks like a simple fishing pole with a piece of denim dangling from the end of a string. Don't be fooled by how simple it appears. The pole is made of fiberglass that is strong enough to bend so the pole won't snap in half yet is very light to handle. The string is a heavy gauge fishing line with a little piece of denim at the end. The reason I usually choose the Kitty Tease over other fishing pole toys is that the denim on the end is small and non-threatening to a cat. Some of the other fishing pole toys have huge colorful toys on the end. For a nervous cat a large toy flung down next to him will be more frightening than enticing. The small denim piece on the end of the Kitty Tease will catch your cat's eye without intimidating him. The Kitty Tease is available in many pet supply stores and by mail order from the manufacturer. See the Appendix for the address of the Galkie Company. Replacement string is also available. Always store this toy away when playtime is over.

The Cat Dancer is my other standard Play Therapy equipment. This black wire has a tightly rolled brown paper toy on the end. The wire causes the toy on the end to move unpredictably. Just by barely moving the wire you can cause the toy to move like a bug flying around, going in every direction. The Cat Dancer is great for cats needing some good exercise. This toy is also very inexpensive. Because the wire can be curled up it's an easy toy to stash away in a drawer or other convenient spot . Then you can get to it quickly to distract an aggressive cat about to pounce on an unsuspecting companion cat (more on this later in the chapter). The Cat Dancer is sold in almost every pet supply store and is available in mail-order catalogs. If you're unable to locate one, I've listed the manufacturer's address in the Appendix. Ask your local store to order it. As with the Kitty Tease, store the Cat Dancer away when you're through with Play Therapy.

For a toy that will fly like a real bird, get Da Bird by Go Cat Feather Toys. This interactive toy has feathers on the end that twirl around as you move it through the air. I recommend Da Bird if you're trying to turn an outdoor cat into an indoor one because he'll feel as if he's still catching birds. This toy is incredibly fun and is a must for obese cats.

A peacock feather is a great toy for your cat. Don't annoy him by brushing it across his face, but use it on the floor nearby to attract him to its light movements. You can also dangle it in the air to encourage your kitty to reach. A peacock feather isn't a replacement for the Kitty Tease or Cat Dancer but rather it's an additional tool for bored cats.

How to Play

For nervous and timid cats use the Kitty Tease exclusively in the beginning. For aggressive, bored, obese or other cats you can use this toy combined with the Cat Dancer and Da Bird. For both, the method of play will be similar.

Play Therapy with the Kitty Tease or Cat Dancer consists of you reawakening the predatory instinct in your cat. Many people fail when it comes to playing with cats because they just toss toys (such as a catnip-filled mouse) on the floor. The cat plays with it initially and then loses interest. After a few paw swipes the toy essentially becomes "dead" prey. Cats are attracted to movement. Cats in the wild can sight a little field mouse sneaking through tall blades of grass, so the amount of movement needed to attract your indoor cat to play can be very subtle. Dangling the Cat Dancer or Kitty Tease in your cat's face isn't the way to entice him. All you'll accomplish is to annoy or frighten him.

With your interactive toy in hand, imagine yourself to be a little mouse trapped inside the house. With that in mind, react with the toy in the way a mouse would. The frightened mouse certainly wouldn't run right up to the cat and say "Here I am!" He'd look for cover— perhaps hiding behind a table leg. Then maybe he'd make a mad dash for the couch. And, because we're dealing with a tiny mouse brain, remember to make some tactical errors to allow your cat to become intrigued with the game. For instance: in an effort to run from behind the chair to beneath the coffee table, our "mouse" runs out in the open and then freezes. Petrified, he quivers in one spot, hoping the cat hasn't seen him. By this time you should be noticing your cat slinking toward your make-believe mouse, preparing for an ambush.

The most important factor in Play Therapy regarding your cat's self-confidence will be making sure he has success as a hunter. Don't frustrate him by never allowing him several captures. And, always end the game on a positive note by allowing him one final grand victory. He'll walk away from the game feeling better about himself.

The first few times you attempt to entice a normally hard-core sedentary cat, don't expect miracles. If the most you get is a glimmer of interest in the eyes, or you notice the ears pricked forward, then you've had a successful session.

For nervous cats, schedule playtime at a quiet time of the day, away from all the household noise and traffic. Later on you'll want to play with him surrounded by normal household noise so he can get used to those sounds while distracting him and keeping him confident with the Play Therapy. But for now, don't overwhelm your cat. Building self-esteem will involve getting him to the point of trusting enough to stop worrying about his environment so he can concentrate on playtime. The Kitty Tease is a good toy to start with because it's quiet and you have a great deal of control. You can also use the peacock feather.

As the cat becomes more confident you can introduce the Cat Dancer for variation. Play Therapy sessions should be done at least twice a day (morning and night). Eventually, when your cat is secure, each session should last about fifteen minutes. But to start, be satisfied with a couple of minutes and gradually work up in time.

For aggressive cats, use either the Cat Dancer or the Kitty Tease. Do one fifteen-minute session in the morning and one in the evening. I know you're wondering how you're going to fit this into your already busy schedule but a half hour a day is a small price to pay for a happy, well adjusted cat. The reason I've picked fifteen minutes is to allow the cat to fully enjoy the session, releasing all of his tension and ending the session feeling satisfied and calm. If you play with an aggressive or high-strung cat for just four or five minutes you'll be leaving him in a highly excited state which will intensify behavior problems. Sometimes aggression for seemingly no reason toward people is just the result of boredom. Regular Play Therapy sessions can stop that.

Use your interactive toys to help avoid fights in multicat households. Stash away a few Cat Dancers in strategic spots around the house. Then, if you're sitting in the living room watching TV one night and you see your resident bully stalking an unsuspecting cat you can reach for the Cat Dancer. Use the toy to distract the aggressor away from the other cat. The aggressor will play with the Cat Dancer, release his tension, forget about his original victim, and everyone's happy. All cats involved are left with a positive memory which helps bring them closer to acceptance.

Obese and sedentary cats especially need regularly scheduled Play Therapy sessions. Even if your fat cat just rolls on his side and casually paws at the Cat Dancer, consider it progress. Each session he'll get more involved.

Instruct other family members how to use the interactive toys (these toys will help accelerate acceptance of a new spouse). If you're going out of town and are having a sitter come in to care for your cat, instruct him or her on how to do the Play Therapy sessions. Keeping up the sessions and maintaining a normal routine is important for your cat during your absence.

Other Types of Toys

Your interactive toys are the ones you bring out for Play Therapy and put away when not in use. In the meantime, there are other toys and fun things to leave out for your cat in case he feels the urge to play when you're not around. I've listed a few good choices but use your imagination to come up with other amusing toys. The success of these toys will be based on not letting your cat grow tired of them. Rotate toys on a regular basis.

Ping-Pong Balls
They're light and fun to bat around. Cats love to play kitchen hockey with them. Get an empty tissue box and drop a ping-pong ball inside, and you've created a game that can keep a cat amused. A word of caution: Some cats can bite through the ball and risk getting it caught in their mouth. If your cat bites hard enough to puncture the ball then only provide ping-pong balls under supervision.

Cardboard Boxes
Line one with a towel and use it as a bed or cut holes in a couple and put them together to create a homemade cat condo. Drop a ping-pong ball in one.

Paper Bags

Paper grocery bags are great fun (don't use plastic bags and don't use bags with handles). Occasionally leave one of these bags on the floor before going out to work in the morning. When you have two cats, paper bags are wonderful because when one cat goes in, the sound of rustling paper will attract the other.

Kick Bags

For the aggressive cat who likes to grasp a toy with his front paws and kick it with his hind paws. This catnip-filled bag looks like a stuffed tube sock. Available at pet supply stores.

Catnip-Filled Mice

No self-respecting owner would be caught dead without at least one catnip-filled mouse in the cat's toy basket. Since cats can lose their interest in catnip if exposed to it continually, you're better off buying a mouse without catnip or at least rotating the toy so it's not left around every day. Whatever kind of mouse you buy, be sure to remove all glued parts (such as eyes) that can be easily chewed off and swallowed. My favorite mouse is the Tuff Mouse, available at most pet supply stores. Just remove the tail (it pulls out easily) to make it a safer toy.

Catnip & Its Importance in Behavior Modification

I'm constantly surprised at how many owners never supply catnip for their cats. For well-adjusted cats, catnip is a fun treat; for cats with behavior problems it's a therapeutic necessity.

When a cat is exposed to catnip he becomes harmlessly intoxicated. The effect lasts between 5 and 15 minutes, is completely safe, and it is not addictive. The main constituent of catnip is nepetalactone which is an oil in the leaves. It's believed that cats react to the nepetalactone because it resembles a chemical in tomcat urine. Both male and female cats during catnip exposure assume positions resembling females in heat (something females in estrus do when they come across the scent of tomcat urine).

You'll notice your cat will do a lot of body rolling, face rubbing and head shaking. He'll rub his head over the catnip, sniffing, licking and chewing (chewing catnip leaves is completely safe). The skin on his back may even twitch a bit as he becomes more intoxicated.

The reason I use catnip as a regular part of therapy is that it provides such ecstasy for a cat. This is a much needed experience for a cat who has been tense and nervous or bored and depressed. This is a wonderful way to get overweight, sedentary cats to kick up their heels a little. Although the initial reaction to catnip will appear stimulating, your cat will then become satiated and relaxed.

You can either buy dried catnip or you can grow your own from seeds. If you choose to buy it, look for good quality catnip that says on the label that only blossoms and leaves are used (it'll be more potent). Brands that use stems in their catnip are generally of a lower quality (and less potent). Buy catnip at pet supply stores for a better selection. Don't buy the kind sold in the supermarket.

You can grow catnip from seeds. Catnip is a perennial with white and lavender blossoms. The plant will reach a height of about three feet. If you decide to grow it outside in the garden be sure you protect it from outdoor cats or your yard will be the most popular one in the neighborhood. I grow it indoors in a window box planter. With some cats, though, you may need to keep it out of reach and only allow scheduled exposure (some cats will knock a whole planter over). The seed packet will have instructions on when to harvest. To dry the catnip you can spread the leaves out on paper or a flat baking sheet and store in a dry place for three to five days.

You can also dry the plant by hanging it in small bunches upside down in a dry place. When dried, pick out and discard the stems. Store the leaves in a tightly sealed glass jar out of your cat's reach. Don't store it in a plastic bag because your cat will make short work of it, and you'll end up having to vacuum up quite a mess. Don't crumble the leaves when you put them in the jar if you can help it . Crumbling releases the aromatic oils, so save that for when you're ready to use it.

Don't rely on catnip-filled toys from stores for your source of catnip. The quality of catnip used is questionable (and sometimes it isn't even catnip at all). Buy loose catnip or grow your own and then you can put some in an old sock and create your own catnip toy. You can also rub some on a toy mouse. You don't even have to do anything with the catnip other than sprinkle some on a paper plate and put it on the floor. Your cat will roll all over it and have a great time.

If you leave catnip around every day for your cat he'll become desensitized to its effects. So limit catnip "parties" to twice a week and when the good time is over put any remaining catnip away. Don't leave catnip-scented toys around.

Catnip is a wonderful way to get a cat out of his shell or to help him forget about his worries for a little while. Don't overlook this gift that nature has provided. Intensity of reaction to catnip can vary. Some cats become mildly intoxicated and others go into sheer ecstasy. Kittens don't respond to catnip at all. There are also some adult cats who just don't react to its effect either. So don't think your cat's strange if you've tried catnip and he doesn't care for it.

In some male cats (especially intact males) it can bring out a more aggressive play behavior. So it's important to watch your cat the first time you give him catnip. You need to determine if he's going to be one of those aggressive types, because in a multicat household he could attempt to play too aggressively with others.

In addition to twice-a-week catnip parties, I also provide it as a treat after stressful times (like vet visits, loud visitors in the house, etc.). If you plan to travel and are having a sitter care for your cat, instruct him or her on how to treat your cat to catnip in order to ease his loneliness and anxiety during your absence.

chapter 5

Eating Behavior

ats have us well trained. I have owners calling me all the time, telling me how finicky their cats are. They complain how at mealtime they'll very often have to open three or four different cans of food before their cats will decide to eat. "Valentine will only eat chicken-flavored canned food in the morning...opened fresh from the can...if I put a little chopped egg on top...served in one of my good china dishes...while I sing to her." That's just about the kind of ritual many owners put themselves through, believing their cats are finicky, fussy eaters. Yes, cats certainly do have people well trained.

Like children who hold out for dessert, or pizza instead of broccoli, cats who have been trained to hold out for the tastier stuff by turning up their nose at what's first offered will definitely use that knowledge. Many people believe that cats are born finicky. They think it's part of their job as owners to go through several kinds of food on a daily basis while kitty makes her choice. We've unintentionally made our cats finicky so they've learned to rely on their taste buds instead of their nutritional needs.

I know you breathe a sigh of relief when you see your finicky eater happily munching away at her favorite food but it may not be the best food for her. Some pet food manufacturers know what will make their food more palatable and they use those ingredients to lure the cat. Don't buy food based solely on your cat's taste buds. Consider her nutritional needs and health first.

Cats are true carnivores. While you may choose a vegetarian lifestyle, don't assume it's healthier for your cat also. Cats aren't able to convert beta-carotene into vitamin A the way we can. They must get vitamin A from animal tissue (called preformed A). Cats are also unable to convert linoleic acid (an essential fatty acid) to arachidonic acid the way dogs can so they must get preformed arachidonic acid from its only source—animal tissue. "Essential" fatty acids aren't manufactured by the body and must be obtained through diet.

Tuna isn't good for your cat. The vegetable oil in tuna is polyunsaturated fat, which is too difficult for a cat to metabolize. (Remember a cat isn't a furry little human. Just because polyunsaturated fat is better for us, it doesn't mean it's healthier for a cat.) Tuna is also high in mineral salts that can form bladder stones.

The taste and smell of tuna are very strong and have an addictive effect on cats. Many people mistakenly believe that all cats are born fishermen and that they need fish in their diets. Tuna robs the cat's body of vitamin E. If enough of this vitamin is depleted the cat becomes at risk of developing a painful condition called "steatitis." This condition causes the fat in a cat's body to become hard. The first visible signs include a greasy, dull coat. Then lumps of fat begin to develop under the skin. As the condition progresses the cat becomes extremely sensitive to being touched and movement is painful. A cat who becomes a tuna junkie will eventually refuse to eat anything else. It's not unusual for tuna-addicted cats to be nervous or aggressive. By following the recommendations in this chapter you'll be able to wean your cat off tuna and back onto a healthy, well-balanced diet.

Milk is another food that many people believe a cat needs. After weaning, a kitten loses the enzyme needed to digest the carbohydrate sugar in milk. The sugar is called lactose. I'm sure you've heard the term "lactose intolerant." Adult cats can develop diarrhea from milk. If your cat doesn't have trouble digesting milk, a little now and then is okay, but certainly not on a regular basis. Plain yogurt is a better treat if you want to supply an extra source of calcium from dairy.

Cats need cat food, not dog food. Feeding dog food to your cat can result in some serious health complications. Cats require more protein and fat in their diets than dogs. Feeding the wrong food will cause a deficiency. Feeding cat food to your dog is also dangerous. The higher protein can lead to kidney problems and the higher fat content can lead to obesity. Cats also require the amino acid taurine in their diet since they're unable to synthesize it in their bodies the way dogs can. Cat food is fortified with taurine specifically for this need.

Don't feed baby food (something many owners mistakenly believe is a perfect diet for their cats). Baby food doesn't have the correct nutrient requirements needed by a cat and can create health problems.

Table scraps are also an unacceptable diet for a cat. They're not well balanced and lack the specific nutrients required to maintain feline health. Table scraps are also often too rich and spicy; this can cause gastrointestinal problems.

Proper diet affects health and behavior. The right nutrition can mean the difference between an even temperament, a shiny coat, and a higher resistance to disease, or a dull, greasy coat, nervousness and a compromised immune system.

Each cat's individual health and nutritional requirements need to be evaluated. That means a cat with any special health condition should be on a diet prescribed by your vet. These conditions include kidney disease, diabetes, allergies, obesity, etc. Monitoring your cat is important because as she ages or as her health changes her dietary requirements will change as well. Work with your veterinarian when it comes to a cat with special health considerations. If your vet recommends a prescription formula then follow his or her instructions. The cost of the prescription food is far less than the cost of hospitalizing a cat with an advanced medical condition.

If your cat is in good health then she needs a top quality nutritional program aimed at keeping her in top form. Your vet can recommend some good brands and the appropriate formulas for your cat's age. Remember, kittens need a growth formula to ensure they get the extra protein and nutrients a sprouting feline needs.

Water

Fresh water must be available at all times. Don't use tap water because of the metals and contaminants that may be present. If you live in an area with hard water then your cat will be getting an increased amount of minerals in her water. I prefer bottled spring water. You can also use distilled water. Change the water daily and wash the bowl even if your cat doesn't finish it. Fresh clean water is much more appealing.

Cats drink water by curling the sides of their tongue and using it as a ladle. Some cats dip their paws in the water and then lick the moisture from them. This method is a form of play for some cats and for others it may just have become a habit. Whatever method your cat uses is unimportant as long as she does drink. For paw dippers, keep the water changed often because you don't want it becoming contaminated by whatever little nasties are on the bottom of her paws.

Retraining the Finicky Eater

If a cat who has never been a finicky eater starts rejecting her food, have your vet do an exam. Several medical conditions can cause a cat to lose her appetite—gingivitis, an abscess, illness, respiratory ailment, lower urinary tract disease, fever. If your vet prescribes a special diet, stick with it and don't offer any other food to your cat. And in general, it's a good idea to check with your vet before making dietary changes and including supplementation because he or she knows your individual cat's specific medical history.

If your cat has a healthy appetite, eats a high-quality diet, but loses weight, be sure she's checked by the vet. It doesn't even have to be a serious illness that causes the weight loss; it could be parasites. The vet can examine your cat and do a fecal check to detect worms or other parasites.

Okay, now for the retraining. I warn you in advance, it's going to be tough. Your cat is going to pull out all of the stops to make you feel guilty. She's going to meow, cry, plead, look pitiful, roll over on her side and feign starvation, attempt to charm you with affection, stare you down, convince you that she feels unloved, and maybe even look at the can opener longingly. Be prepared. For retraining to be a success you've got to be convinced you're doing what's best for your cat and that in the end she'll be happier and healthier. In the meantime, though, invest in a pair of earplugs.

Rule number one: Buy only good quality cat food. There are several brands available from your vet or from pet supply stores. I prefer to stay away from supermarket brands because many are loaded with artificial preservatives, flavorings and colors. In some cases the quality of the protein isn't high enough and some manufacturers aren't above using things like tuna and other strong-tasting foods to entice your cat to eat. Although you may feel that the premium foods cost more, they're *nutrient dense* and that means a cat won't have to eat as much to meet her nutritional requirements.

Many of the supermarket brands are designed to be palatable to the cat and appealing to the owner. How many times have you opened one of the supermarket brands and thought it resembled human food—all those nice, uniform slices of meat or the evenly diced pieces that are the perfect color, or beef surrounded by a rich gravy? Cats don't care about that stuff but pet food manufacturers know that we do. We somehow feel that we're feeding our precious kitty a better food if it looks more like what we'd serve ourselves. The truth is, the prremium brands (such as Science Diet, Iams, Pro Plan, Wysong, and Nature's Recipe) are formulated specifically with the cat's true nutritional needs in mind. So before you begin to retrain your finicky eater you need to arm yourself with the proper tool—nutrition!

If you've been leaving food available free choice, I suggest you take it up and start adjusting your cat to scheduled meals. Food in the wild isn't available all day. The digestive system needs a chance to rest. Also, during meals the cat's urine is more alkaline. *Acidic* urine is what helps dissolve the urinary calculi that lead to cystitis and lower urinary tract disease. By not leaving food available all the time you'll encourage a healthier appetite. Food should be left down for about fifteen to twenty minutes (with an absolute maximum of a half hour). After that time it should be removed (even if food has been left un-eaten) and only fresh water made available. Call your cat into the room when you serve her dinner so she'll start getting acquainted with the new meal schedule.

If you're changing over to a new food, gradually introduce it by mixing a small amount in with your cat's regular brand. Increase the amount of the new food a little each time over the next week to ten days. This way your cat won't object to the change. She may even take to this food right away without any complaints. A gradual intro-duction of new food also helps to avoid any intestinal upset.

Alternate canned and dry food. Since dry food contributes more toward LUTD (lower urinary tract disease), buy only a top quality professional brand. That way you'll know it's lower in magnesium (the main culprit in LUTD). I also feel the variety helps prevent finicky eating. I believe a diet of all canned or all dry isn't as healthy. Now I know some of you have been told that canned food contributes to tooth decay and that dry food helps clean teeth. Dry food does keep the teeth a little cleaner, but I've seen many cats who have been on dry food exclusively and they have had the worst cases of gum dis-ease. If you're really concerned about maintaining your cat's dental health, purchase a toothpaste made especially for pets and brush your cat's teeth (see Chapter 8 for more on this).

Unless your veterinarian instructs you otherwise, feed your cat twice a day. Now I can hear you complaining already about how inconvenient that will be and how you can't always get home from work in time to feed your cat her dinner. If your hours are irregular feed as close to a normal schedule as you can. Your cat will soon adjust and if dinner is a half hour late she'll know not to panic. If maintaining somewhat of a normal schedule is completely impossible, then you'll have to leave food free choice.

Retraining a finicky eater is important. Even if she's healthy now, at some point in her life she may need to be on a special diet for a medical condition. Feeding a good quality food on a scheduled basis will also help do away with some present unpleasantness you and your cat may be enduring, such as greasy coat, dandruff, obesity or lethargy.

To help encourage your cat's appetite, simulate what happens in the wild when a cat goes looking for food. Since a hunt and chase must usually precede a meal, play with your cat to get her digestive juices flowing. When you come home from work at night your cat has probably spent a great deal of her day sleeping so a good game of hunting is just what her sluggish circulation needs (refer to chapter 4 for tips on playtime). After playtime, reward your cat with a healthy, nourishing meal. Then when the fifteen to twenty minutes are up, remove the food (unless of course she's just a slow eater and is still working on her dinner). Once dinner is over, don't sneak any treats to your kitty if she hasn't eaten. She's probably holding out because she knows that in the past she's been able to con you into providing something deliciously sinful. Be strong!

Serve food at room temperature so it'll be its most appealing. Take it out of the refrigerator and allow it to come to room temperature while you engage in playtime with your cat. For very finicky eaters or elderly cats with a decreased sense of smell you can warm moist food in the microwave to release the aroma. Heat only a meal-size portion. Reheating food twice will destroy precious nutrients. Serving cold food can cause gastric upset in addition to being unappealing.

If you have more than one cat provide each with his or her food bowl. Use glass or stainless steel instead of plastic. Some cats have allergic reactions to plastic bowls. Teaching cats to eat only out of their own bowls can give them a sense of security because they'll no longer have to worry about a more dominant cat pushing her way into another bowl. Training cats to their own bowls also has the advantage of allowing you to provide specific diets to each cat as needed and gives you the opportunity to monitor just how much food each cat is eating. In a multicat household if all the cats eat out of a community bowl you have no way of knowing if someone isn't eating until the physical symptom of weight loss appears.

Beneficial Supplementation

With high quality brands of food you don't really need to supplement. Still, there are a couple of additives that can be especially useful for cats going through behavioral or health problems. Even a healthy cat can benefit from these ingredients.

Dry Mix
    1 cup nutritional, brewer's, or tarula yeast
    1 cup oat or wheat bran
    2 cups lecithin granules
Mix all of the ingredients together and store in a covered container in the refrigerator. Having it all mixed together makes it very convenient to add to each meal. Add one-half to one full teaspoon (depending on your cat's size) to each moist meal (for a maximum of two teaspoons per cat per day). I emphasize mixing it in with the canned food and not the dry food because when you're taking bran into the body there has to be adequate moisture to go with it.

The ingredients in the dry mix perform a number of beneficial functions.

Bran
Bran supplies fiber. All cats, especially long-haired ones, need a good amount of dietary roughage to do away with hairballs. The added roughage in the diet helps maintain good colon health and is of extra benefit to obese cats.

Brewer's Yeast
A source of amino acids and B vitamins. Cats under stress (and any cat with a behavior problem is under stress) use up so much vitamin B. This wonderful vitamin is also easily destroyed in the processing of canned food. Cats usually love the taste so it also helps those finicky eaters. Brewer's yeast does have magnesium in it so if your cat is suffering from LUTD (lower urinary tract disease) omit this from the dry mix.

Lecithin
Those of you who have read my book, *Cat Love,* may notice that I've doubled the amount of lecithin. This remarkable supplement emulsifies fatty wastes, virtually eliminates dandruff and creates a stunning coat. Since so many cats seem to have either dull greasy coats or dry

brittle coats loaded with dandruff, their need for lecithin is much greater. By increasing the amount of lecithin I've seen glorious results.

Note: Bone meal is a supplement I will include in the dry mix if I feel the cat needs the extra calcium (ask your vet first). The amount to add to the mix is one-quarter cup. Be sure it's bone meal and not dolomite because dolomite doesn't have the correct ratio of calcium and phosphorus. If you're feeding your cat one of the premium cat foods (such as Science Diet, Iams, Natural Life, Wysong, Nature's Recipe) then she's getting enough calcium from the diet and you don't need to include the bone meal. When buying bone meal be *absolutely* sure of its quality because so much is contaminated with lead. All of the ingredients are available in natural food stores. To get your cat used to the addition of the dry mix, start by introducing a tiny amount (about one-eighth teaspoon or less) and gradually increase. Always add the dry mix fresh to each meal. Don't mix a bunch of it into an entire can of food that's going to be stored in the refrigerator. The effects of the dry mix are better if it's added fresh each time.

Vitamin C

This water-soluble vitamin isn't stored in the body. It is needed in larger amounts during times of stress and emotional turmoil. Vitamin C may also help acidify the urine which can decrease your cat's chances of developing LUTD. Vitamin C is also a wonderful healing vitamin. I use it for cats recovering from illness or injury. Since this vitamin is acidic you need to completely crush it and mix it into the food. You don't want to pop a vitamin C pill down your cat's throat because it could irritate the esophagus. I crush a 100mg tablet and mix it into a moist meal (never a dry food meal) as needed. If you feed two moist meals that day you can divide the vitamin so you're giving 50mg in the morning meal and 50mg in the evening meal. For maintenance I use vitamin C two to three times a week. During crisis situations I'll include it daily on a temporary basis. I also extend a cat's intake of this vitamin to include a few days before and a few days after a vet visit (especially if tests, X rays, or surgery are being done). On the days when you're not supplementing the meal with vitamin C you can add a teaspoon of tomato juice to the moist food to help keep the urine acidic. Once you open the can transfer the contents to a glass container or else it will develop a metallic taste. Keep refrigerated.

Vitamin B Complex

The B complex vitamin is also not stored by the body. Just as with vitamin C, it's needed in times of stress. Crush 10-15mgs into moist food during emotional upheavals. Since a 10-15mg tablet is virtually impossible to find, buying a capsule is easiest. This way you can open the capsule and divide the powder inside. I know you won't be able to be totally accurate with your measurement but try to approximate 10-15mgs and store the unused amount in a small vial or, if you can, reclose the capsule.

Vitamin E
If you're trying to reform a tuna junkie your cat truly needs some added vitamin E in her diet. Prick a 200IU capsule and squeeze the contents into a meal two to three times a week while you're weaning her off tuna.

Multivitamin Supplements
I don't give vitamin supplements on a daily basis because I feed a good quality diet and I don't want my cat's system to depend on a little pill for nutrients. If I do give a vitamin it's on an irregular basis. The only supplementation I do on a daily basis is the dry mix. Depending on your cat's age and health, your vet may recommend a multivitamin supplement.

Vegetables
I sometimes add a small amount of vegetables to my cats' meals to increase fiber and water content. Veggies are also beneficial for over-weight cats because it takes them longer to eat and they feel more satisfied. I don't add vegetables every day because a good quality cat food is complete and balanced, but when I do add some my cats sure do love them. Good vegetable choices include: shredded carrot, chopped celery (remove any stringy parts), chopped cucumber, chopped alfalfa sprouts, chopped broccoli, and chopped zucchini.

Good Treats

Brewer's Yeast Tablets
Keep a jar of brewer's yeast tablets on hand to use as rewards for good behavior. Substitute these for any of the commercial treats you may have been using before. Don't feed a handful, just one. Cats love this tablet form of the same brewer's yeast that you include in the food.

Cantaloupe Ball
An occasional cantaloupe ball is a fun toy and many cats find them tasty.

Raw Green Bean
Cats love to play with them.

Grapes

Another fun toy for cats. Some will eat the grape after playing with it but most will proceed to lose it under furniture.

Yogurt

If you want to give your cat a dairy treat, give a tablespoon of plain, unflavored yogurt instead of milk.

Bad Treats

Table scraps

Eliminate all table scraps from your cat's diet. In addition to being too rich and spicy, they throw off the balance of the diet. Your cat won't want to eat her cat food if she knows she can hold out for a bite of your hamburger. Feeding table scraps also encourages begging which isn't acceptable behavior in felines.

Sweets

Cats in general don't have a sweet tooth but we often make the mistake of providing enough nibbles of our desserts that a taste for sweets develops. Cats certainly don't need all that sugar. The most dangerous of all is chocolate. It contains theobromine which is highly toxic to cats and can be deadly. What seems like a small amount to you can actually be lethal to your small pet. Don't ever give your cat or dog chocolate of any kind.

Bones

A cat's teeth can easily break while trying to chew on a bone. Some small bones (such as chicken) can splinter and get lodged in the cat's throat or pierce the intestines. Keep all bones away from cats. If you throw chicken bones in the garbage, make sure there's no way your cat can get at them.

Obesity

If you're unsure as to whether your cat is overweight or not, consult your veterinarian. He or she will be able to advise you on the ideal weight for your cat based on her age, health, and activity level. He or she will also be able to provide you with weight loss guidelines. That is, how much your cat should lose and the proper amount of food (and types of food) to accomplish this. Obesity isn't always the result of overeating; it can be caused by a metabolic disorder. If you're concerned about your cat's weight it's best to have her examined.

Gaining or losing a couple of pounds is a bigger deal for a cat than it is for a human because a pound is a larger percentage of her overall body weight. Losing weight too rapidly can result in hepatic lipidosis which is a serious liver condition. Your vet will be able to provide you with specific weight loss guidelines but generally a 20-30% decrease in food is the maximum amount you'd want to cut from her diet. As with humans, an increased activity level during dieting is an important factor (refer to Chapter 4 for tips on playtime).

If you leave food available free choice and your cat is overweight, then feeding a good quality diet, providing exercise, and removing food between mealtimes should be your new routine.

Another option to cutting back on your cat's regular food is to switch to one of the lighter formulas. They're lower in fat and have a higher fiber level. There are several brands available (such as Science Diet Feline Maintenance Light, Pro Plan Light, Iams Less Active). Depending upon the amount of weight your cat needs to lose, your vet may recommend one of the prescription diet formulas (such as Hill's r/d or w/d). If you use one of the commercial foods you can add the dry mix into the moist meals. The lecithin is especially beneficial during weight loss as it helps emulsify fatty wastes. If you use a prescription formula like r/d or w/d, omit the bran from the dry mix because the food has enough fiber. The brewer's yeast and lecithin are very beneficial, though.

During a feline weight loss program your kitty will have to do without those special little treats you've managed to slip to her in the past. No more pieces of bacon, bites of pizza, slices of pepperoni, or slivers of cheese. If you absolutely insist on giving her a special treat then choose a low cal one like a slice of cucumber or a teaspoon of plain yogurt.

Be sure to provide lots of fresh clean spring water (or distilled) to help all the extra fiber in her diet do its wonderful job.

While we're on the subject of obesity, I'd like to straighten out some incorrect information. Many people believe all neutered and spayed cats get fat. The truth is, neutered and spayed cats are less inclined to roam so they may become a little less active. To avoid obesity, just feed less than you would to an intact cat.

During weight loss, provide your cat with lots of extra love and praise. Compliment her during playtime as you watch her become more athletic and confident. I know you're probably thinking I'm nuts to tell you to compliment your cat but the tone of your voice will have a positive effect on her.

Anorexia

Cats can suffer from anorexia for many reasons. For example, during an upper respiratory infection the nasal passages become blocked. Because the cat is unable to smell the food, she stops eating. Warming the food to release more of the aroma may help. Garlic and brewer's yeast, both of which have a strong taste, may also be of help. If ever your cat stops eating for more than two days you need to have her examined by the vet. He or she will provide you with specific instructions on caring for an anorexic cat. Once the cause of the anorexia is diagnosed, your vet may prescribe a special food, such as Hill's a/d which is a highly palatable formula to spark your cat's appetite. The liquid consistency of a/d makes it convenient for syringe feeding. Your vet may also prescribe Nutrical, which is a high caloric and nutritional supplement in paste form. Valium is also sometimes used as an appetite stimulant.

Anorexia can also be the result of a psychological trauma. When dealing with a cat suffering from such a trauma, be sure her meals are served in a quiet area, use the Bach Flower Remedies (such as Star of Bethlehem and Hornbeam), and if she'll eat at all, add the C and B vitamins.

Allergies

If your vet determines that your cat may have a food allergy you'll be instructed to put her on a prescribed diet (usually a lamb and rice formula). Keep your cat on this diet as long as your vet recommends. Don't feed anything other than the prescribed food. The purpose of this diet is to eliminate anything that could be causing the allergy. Your vet may gradually have you add individual foods back into the diet to try to determine which food is causing the reaction.

For a cat with any kind of allergy (whether it's to a food, dust, pollen, etc.), create a supportive and healthy environment by:
• purifying the air with an ionizer/air purifier
• eliminating the use of aerosol room fresheners
• not exposing your cat to cigarette, cigar or pipe smoke
• keeping your cat on a good quality food that doesn't have all those unnecessary additives
• providing regular Play Therapy sessions
• making sure your cat has a cozy bed away from high traffic, dust-raising areas
• if pollen is the problem, keeping windows closed during peak seasons
• using the Bach Flower Remedy, Crab Apple, to help detoxify (give 4 drops 4 times a day when needed)
• controlling the flea population in and around your home to avoid allergic reactions to flea bites

- using only distilled water
- not using fabric softener in your laundry (especially on sheets and comforters that your cat may sleep on).

Feeding the Older Cat

As your cat enters her golden years her dietary needs change. Less protein is required (so as not to overwork the kidneys) but the quality of the protein needs to remain high. Also, older cats sometimes do better with smaller meals fed more frequently.

If you've been treating your cat to special tidbits of table scraps, that really needs to cease as she ages. Her body won't be able to process that piece of pepperoni the way it did when she was younger. You need to think in terms of easing the work load on her digestive system, kidneys, liver, heart, and all the other parts that have been going full steam all these years. Though she may still look and act like the same young cat to you, her dietary requirements may need a little fine tuning. And speaking of fine tuning, those routine visits to the vet are even more important as your kitty gets older. Catching any subtle changes in her health or behavior early will greatly increase her chances of having many more happy years of retirement.

Provide plenty of fresh spring or distilled water instead of tap water. An aging cat's system doesn't need to be doing all that extra work to filter any rust or contaminants from the water.

As the digestive enzymes diminish with age, your cat might benefit from the addition of some digestive enzymes. Very Healthy Enterprises makes a Feline Digestive Enzyme Formula to help a cat utilize more of the nutrients from her food (the manufacturer's address is in the Appendix). Your vet may also have a specific recommendation for a digestive enzyme formula. Consult your vet before supplementing with digestive enzymes to be sure they're right for your cat's specific condition.

Include the dry mix in your older cat's food because the extra fiber is needed as the digestive system gets sluggish. The lecithin will also help with dandruff problems that many older cats get.

Vitamin C (100mg) two or three times a week will help keep a senior kitty's resistance up. Your vet may even prescribe a multivitamin at this point for your cat if she needs the extra help.

Sometimes older cats need a little enticement to eat. Try warming the food slightly to release more of the aroma. Some cats like the strong taste of garlic so you can try chopping up a tiny bit and mixing it in the food. Using the dry mix will also help because the brewer's yeast in it increases the taste. Don't weaken and resort to sneaking bad treats into the food such as tuna, bacon, or last night's leftover meatloaf.

Feeding the Nervous or Timid Cat

Where you feed the nervous or timid cat is very important. Her meals should be served in a quiet area away from all the household traffic. You can't expect her to feel comfortable and relaxed enough to enjoy her dinner if the children are running in and out of the kitchen or the family dog is attempting to steal a few nibbles. Feed in a peaceful area at a quiet time so your cat doesn't have to feel threatened. Some cats in busy households prefer to eat in an elevated spot. If you live in a multicat household and one cat is repeatedly feeling threatened by a more dominant cat then it helps to feed the cats in separate locations.

Some nervous cats like to have their owners close by while they eat dinner. Your cat may prefer having the comfort of your company during her meals.

Some supplements that may benefit a nervous kitty are vitamin B (10-15mg) and vitamin C (100mg) crushed into a moist meal two or three times a week. Another good addition is to empty the contents of a bee pollen capsule into the food two or three times a week. Chamomile has a relaxing effect, so you can try adding a teaspoon of the leaves into a moist meal. Don't forget the dry mix!

Refer to Chapter 9 for details on nervous personalities.

Feeding the Aggressive Cat

Refer to Chapter 8 for details on aggressive personalities. Food aggression is also covered in that chapter.

Don't feed supermarket foods with all those artificial preservatives, colors and flavors to an aggressive cat. Those packets of semi-moist foods are also out.

Include 10-15mg of vitamin B crushed into a moist meal two to three times a week as needed. 1/4 teaspoon of chamomile tea leaves mixed into the food can also help during aggressive phases. Add the dry mix daily.

Unusual Eating Behaviors

Chewing House Plants

A cat may chew on a house plant to help get rid of hairballs. Some cats also just do it out of boredom. If your cat has a history of vomiting up hairballs, use a hairball remedy (available from your vet or a pet supply store). Be sure to include the dry mix in her moist meals. For bored cats, include lots of playtime to add more spice to life.

This is a serious problem because so many plants are poisonous. If possible, keep plants out of a cat's reach by using hanging planters. Before buying new plants, become familiar with the safest ones to have around pets.

The following is a list of some of the plants that are poisonous:

Apricot	Jerusalem Cherry
Amaryllis	Larkspur
Azalea	Lily of the Valley
Belladonna	Marigold
Box	Marijuana
Bird of Paradise	Morning Glory
Caladium	Nettle
Calla Lily	Nutmeg
Daffodil	Oleander
Dieffenbachia	Peach
English Holly	Philodendron
English Ivy	Pokeweed
Ficus	Potato
Foxglove	Pothos
Hemlock	Schefflera
Honeysuckle	Spider Plant
Hydrangea	Tobacco
Iris	Tulip
Jack-in-the Pulpit	Wisteria
Japanese Yew	

If your cat does ingest a poisonous plant, contact a veterinarian immediately for instructions.

To make plants less desirable to chew, spray bitter apple (available at pet supply stores) on the leaves on a regular basis. The bitter apple spray is made especially for plants so it won't damage the leaves.

Since cats do like to nibble on greenery, grow some wheat or rye grass for her. You can get a kit with everything you need at a pet supply store or you can do it yourself. Wheat berries can be bought at a health food store. Sprinkle the berries in soil (you can use a clay flower pot or any kind of container as long as it's sturdy). Cover lightly with a top layer of about one-quarter inch of soil, keep moist, and soon you'll see grass sprouting up. Keep this home-grown grass available for your cat and she'll prefer it to the house plants. If she still goes for the plants you can use a spray bottle filled with plain water and give her a spritz every time she goes for the plant. In some cases, if a cat continues to insist on chewing the plant, the safest option is just to remove it from the house.

Make sure you're providing enough fiber in your cat's diet by including the dry mix.

Pica
Pica is the behavior of eating non-edible things. A common example of this is a cat who eats litter. Some cats will lick dirt or pavement. Have your vet do a blood test to be sure your cat hasn't developed an anemic condition. If no illness or deficiency is determined as the cause, provide a high quality diet (stay away from supermarket brands), including the dry mix. For treats, use only high fiber, healthy ones like brewer's yeast tablets, cucumber slices, broccoli, a grape, a green bean, or yogurt.

Wool Sucking and Chewing
Wool chewing can have serious complications if enough of the wool accumulates in the stomach. One theory behind wool sucking or chewing is that the scent of lanolin in the wool may resemble the scent of the mother's nipple. Wool chewing is seen most often in Siamese cats.

In many cases I've had success by increasing the fiber in a cat's diet. Including the dry mix will be a good source of fiber in the little wool chewer's diet. In terms of behavior modification, use *distraction* to help the kitty over this phase. Make sure you have interactive toys handy and distract her from the chewing behavior with Play Therapy (chapter 4). For wool suckers, use Play Therapy in combination with lots of affection and attention to build the cat's confidence.

During retraining, instruct all family members not to leave wool clothing around.

Benefits of the Proper Diet

- more playful and active cat (especially as obese cats lose weight)
- increased confidence as coat condition improves and less anti-stress self-grooming is required
- more efficient metabolism (so waste products get eliminated and toxins are cleaned out)
- better disposition
- increased resistance to disease
- longer life
- fresher scent to coat (no fishy smell)
- no finicky eating behavior

chapter 6

Litter Box Problems

The problems I'm called in for most often are litter box related. Litter box problems are very common but they are also very serious and shouldn't be something you just accept as part of being a cat owner.

Cats are very clean animals. Their instinct is to eliminate their waste away from the nest and then bury it to prevent predators from catching the scent. In the wild, this is a matter of life and death. Your domesticated cat has inherited this instinct from his wild ancestors. One of the reasons cats make such popular pets is their fastidious nature and the way they're so easily trained to a litter box. A cat who is driven to urinating or defecating outside the litter box is already so stressed out (if for no other reason than the fact that it goes against that very fastidious nature) and needs your immediate help. Any change in your cat's litter box habits should be viewed as a red flag that something is wrong.

When cats eliminate outside the litter box, the problem is either medical, the litter box (or the litter) itself, or territorial/emotional.

Now that we've identified the possibilities, you'll next have to learn how to determine which problem (or problems) it can be and how to find the solution. Don't worry, I'll guide you through it.

Indiscriminate Urination and Spraying

One very important reason why you might be unsuccessful in dealing with a litter box problem is that you don't understand the difference between indiscriminate urination and spraying. Their causes can be very different. So to find the proper solution, you first have to determine which one your cat is actually doing.

The Evidence

If the wet spot is on a flat surface such as the floor, carpet, bed, chair, sofa, bathtub, in a suitcase, etc., then what you have is indiscriminate urination. If the wet spot is on the side or back of a piece of furniture, stereo speakers, box, door, wall, curtains, etc., or on an item left on the floor (such as a purse or briefcase) then you're dealing with a spraying problem.

A cat indiscriminately urinates outside of the litter box for several reasons. There can be a medical problem; he can be reacting emotionally to a stressful situation—such as a move to a new house, death in the family, new pet, etc.—or it can be that he's not happy with the condition of his litter box and/or its location.

Spraying is usually done for territorial marking. Intact males spray but females sometimes spray if they feel their territory is in danger. Some neutered males may continue to spray if the behavior was too well established before the surgery. A neutered male may also resort to occasional spraying if he feels threatened within his own territory. But in almost all cases, having your cat neutered will eliminate the problem of spraying.

The posture a cat assumes for spraying is very different from the squatting position for normal urination. A cat about to spray will back up to an object, tail held straight up (most times the tail will be twitching). The stream of urine will be directed straight back toward the targeted object.

In the case of multicat households, it can be difficult to determine which cat is actually doing the spraying if you are never able to catch him in the act. One solution is to ask your vet to put fluorescein (an ophthalmic solution that is safe for your cat to take internally) into a capsule and administer to your cat. This liquid will cause the urine to fluoresce. Give the capsule to the cat you most likely suspect as the sprayer. Examining the house with an ultraviolet light will either confirm or eliminate your suspicions about the first cat given the capsule. If no urine is detected with the light, wait a couple of days and give a fluorescein capsule to the next cat.

Litter Box Rejection Due to Medical Problems

When a cat owner calls me and says that his cat has suddenly started urinating outside the litter box, the first thing I say is to get the cat to the vet right away. I'm emphatic about this because the cat could be suffering from cystitis or a urethral blockage (commonly known as FUS, feline urologic syndrome, or LUTD, lower urinary tract disease). This can be a life-threatening situation. Struvite crystals (magnesium-ammonium-phosphate crystals) accumulate in the urinary tract causing irritation. If left untreated, they can eventually block the passage of urine. Excessive magnesium in cat food is known to be the main cause of LUTD. Feeding a good quality, low magnesium diet (such as Science Diet, Iams, Pro Plan, Wysong, to name a few) will greatly reduce your cat's chances of developing LUTD. Nutrition plays a vital role in fighting LUTD. If you have questions about the right diet for your cat, consult your veterinarian. I recommend you stay away from the so called "bargains" found in supermarkets. They often contain excessive amounts of magnesium, preservatives and unnecessary additives. If your vet does diagnose LUTD, a dietary management program will be prescribed. It's imperative that you not sneak that same old supermarket food into your cat's diet as a "treat." You won't be doing him a favor if he ends up with cystitis again.

Indiscriminate urination is usually a common sign of LUTD. The reason you must seek veterinary care immediately is that if the cat does have an infection you have no way of knowing how long it has been going on. Very often the cat will make frequent trips to the litter box and void only small drops of urine each time (sometimes blood-tinged). As the urinary tract lining gets more irritated the cat will feel the need to go whenever and wherever he is to relieve the burning sensation. Sometimes a cat with a urinary tract infection associates the litter box itself with the discomfort he feels each time he tries to void. He may seek another place to urinate in an effort to eliminate the pain (this can also be the case with constipated cats). Since a cat with LUTD usually only voids small drops of urine, chances are you won't even notice that he's urinated on the carpet (especially if it's behind a chair, under the bed or in a closet). By the time you notice that he's not using his box the cat's urinary tract may be almost, if not completely, blocked. This is a fatal situation for a cat. I always feel it's worth the time and money to rush your cat to the vet just to be able to rule out any possible medical problems.

Some signs of LUTD are listed below:
- urination outside the litter box
- frequent trips to the litter box
- straining or crying during urination attempts
- voiding little or no urine
- blood in urine
- frequent licking of genital area
- change in activity level (becoming quiet and depressed)

Many owners mistake the frequent litter box trips and straining/crying as signs of constipation. This is where being an alert owner and monitoring your cat's litter box routine can be a lifesaver. If you notice any of the above signs, see your vet.

Diabetes and kidney disease can also cause a change in your cat's litter box habits. If you notice your cat drinking large quantities of water he could be diabetic. The more water he drinks, the more often he'll need to urinate and it may get to the point where he can't always make it to the box in time. Many older cats suffer from kidney failure that goes unchecked until it reaches a crucial point. Any change in your cat's litter box routine or eating/drinking behavior should be checked by the vet.

Monitor Litter

Early detection of problems like LUTD can mean the difference between a rapid recovery and a prolonged problem. There are some products available to help you stay aware of your cat's medical condition.

The Wysong Medical Corporation makes healthy, natural, environmentally friendly products for pets and people. In addition to special feline and canine diets (including a wonderful hypoallergenic food formula), they make a few litter products that may be of interest to you. One is Litter Lite, which is a dust-free, natural litter, good for sensitive cats with allergies. The other products are the Diagnostic Litter and Diagnostic Pads. The litter and pads are used together to assist in the early detection of changes in urinary pH levels. The special litter, made of compressed cellulose, is designed to allow the urine to pass unaltered to the diagnostic pads below, where it can then be examined for traces of blood and a rise in pH level (indicated by a color change). The Diagnostic Litter is dust-free, non-allergenic and biodegradable. The product also has a natural herbal scent. For LUTD-prone cats you may want to use the litter and pads exclusively. Complete instructions are included with the products. Wysong litter products are available by mail order. Refer to the Appendix for their address.

Cat Scan is a screening system available from your vet. It is sprinkled in the litter box to monitor the status of certain medical conditions. There are four different packets for urine monitoring of blood, pH, glucose, and protein. Being able to monitor a potential or ongoing health problem through this color change system can help you and your vet keep track of your cat's progress.

If your vet gives your cat a clean bill of health you can go home and begin your investigation into why he has rejected his litter box. The place to start is with the box itself.

The Litter Box

A dirty litter box will drive a cat to seek other accommodations, i.e., your carpet, tub, or closet. You must thoroughly clean the box at least once a week. If you have more than one cat you may have to do it twice a week. Just changing the litter will not be enough. If you've been neglecting these duties then there's a good chance your cat has reached the end of his patience and sought another solution. There's just no getting around it, you must clean the box and change the litter as often as needed. It doesn't matter if you use plastic liners. In fact, plastic liners can make a litter box odor problem worse because urine pools in the folds. If you do use plastic liners be sure to get the right size for the box and regularly check if urine is accumulating in corners. Plastic liners can also develop holes in them as your cat scratches in the box. This allows the urine to go underneath the liner and just lie on the bottom of the box. Then what you'll end up with is a pretty smelly box.

The more complicated the whole litter box procedure becomes, the more likely your cat will reject it and the more difficult it will be for you to maintain. Keep things simple: the right box, the right litter, the right location and the right cleaning schedule.

When cleaning the box, use a mild detergent and finish by rinsing very thoroughly. More than one cat has rejected a box that smells too much of disinfectants and strong cleansers. Never use any of those strong-smelling pine cleansers. Ammonia or products containing ammonia shouldn't be used because they closely resemble the odor in urine. Using ammonia can even make a litter box problem worse. If you want to use a disinfectant cleanser or bleach, be sure to dilute it with water first before cleaning the box. Completely rinse every last bit of cleanser off and then dry thoroughly.

To keep the box odor-free between cleanings, you should have a slotted litter shovel and a large plastic spoon to remove the solid wastes and wet clumps. Regularly removing the solids will help prevent a cat from rejecting the box because it's too dirty. It also prevents a cat from having to step on old feces each time he uses the litter box. Removing the wet urine-soaked litter clumps will cut down on odor and keep the box cleaner. Avoid stirring the wet litter into the dry litter because you'll just create a bigger odor problem. You don't want to spread the wet litter all over the box. When your cat steps into the box he's going to want his paws to touch dry litter. A cat will usually urinate in one of the four corners of the box so it should be easy to scoop up a wet clump.

If you have a covered litter box it's especially important that you maintain an adequate cleaning schedule and routinely remove the solids (and hopefully enough of the wet clumps). While the covered box confines the odor to the inside of the box (humans like that idea), it also means that the concentrated odor is trapped in there (which your cat won't be too crazy about). Open boxes allow the litter to dry out, but the litter in covered boxes takes longer to dry. So don't get a covered box unless you're willing to clean it faithfully or you may end up with a cat who refuses to use it.

At different times of the year you may have to adjust the litter box cleaning schedule according to the weather. When the humidity is high, the litter will take longer to dry so it may have to be changed more often.

If you've been responsible in your cleaning duties and you still have a cat that urinates outside the box then take a look at where the box is located in your house. Since the cat's instinct is to bury his waste away from the nest, the box shouldn't be near his bed, food, or water. If you have the box too close to his food, he may also become a poor eater. Make sure the box is located in a quiet, private area. If the box is right in the middle of things there's a good chance he's not too happy with that arrangement. On the other hand, the box shouldn't be placed in such an out-of-the-way area that it becomes too much of an effort for him to get to it in time. This is very important when you're dealing with kittens in training, older cats who have less bladder control, or cystitis-prone cats. If the box is located up or down a stairway then it may have to be moved to a more convenient location in the case of aging or arthritic cats. One simple reason an old cat may refuse to use the box is because it's too painful to climb stairs. If the box is located in a cold basement, an old or arthritic cat may be too uncomfortable.

Moving the litter box around too much can create an indiscriminate urination problem. Find the best spot for the box and don't keep moving it around. If your cat is successfully using the box, leave it there.

If you're moving to a new house, try to put the litter box in the same general location as in your former home. If you used to keep the box in an upstairs bathroom in your old house and you've put it somewhere else in the new house you may find your cat using the new upstairs bathroom. If you can't put the box in relatively the same location in the new house, confine the cat to a smaller area with his box until he's adjusted to the change.

Don't put the litter box on carpet. Many times the texture of the carpet is attractive to the cat as a place to urinate.

What kind of litter box filler you put in the box can itself be the reason your cat has rejected it. There are many kinds of litter box filler—numerous clay types, plain sand, alfalfa pellets, shredded newspaper, sand-like clumping litter, sawdust, pellets made from newspaper, and some people even use soil. The most popular kinds of litter are clay and the sand-like clumping brands. Clay litter is very absorbent and few cats reject it. There are many brands of clay litter available, but, unfortunately, not all are good. If your cat is rejecting his box it may be that you're using a clay litter that's too deodorized. Some cats object to all those strong deodorizing scents that some manufacturers use. If you're concerned about odor control then add some baking soda in with the litter. Baking soda is even better than those commercial deodorizing additives. With most of the deodorizing products you just end up introducing another strong scent into the litter box that your cat may find objectionable. Baking soda is odorless, economical, absorbs odors better than anything else, and is a safe product to use around cats.

Often the cause of a cat rejecting his litter box is that the owner switches brands of litter. Cats are creatures of habit and they don't like abrupt changes. If you must change brands of litter do so very gradually. Mix a little of the new litter in the box with the familiar brand. Gradually increase the amount of new litter each time so your cat can make a smooth adjustment. Once you find a brand of litter that your cat likes, stick with it. Don't buy whatever is on sale each week. It won't end up being such a bargain if your cat starts using the carpet instead of the box.

If you're trying to figure out if it's the litter itself that your cat objects to, have a couple of litter boxes available with different litter in each. You'll soon know which one he prefers.

The popular clumping litter box fillers are a mixed blessing. They have a sand-like consistency and when the cat urinates, the litter holds the moisture in a ball. This makes it easy for you to scoop the dirty litter right out. In theory it seems like a great idea but in reality if you don't scoop up the clumped litter relatively soon it can end up falling apart anyway. Some manufacturers have a harder clumping formula that won't fall apart no matter how aggressively your cat digs. The harder clumping formula can't be flushed though so be sure you read labels before purchasing one of these products to be sure you've picked the appropriate one.

Shredded newspaper as litter box filler is very messy. If your cat is rejecting the litter box it could very well be because newspaper makes for a very odorous box.

As for the other kinds of litter box fillers, sawdust can be very messy and gets tracked everywhere. Soil is bad because a cat may not always know the difference between the soil in his litter box and the soil your favorite plant is sitting in. Besides, soil isn't a clean litter box filler and you'll end up with it dirtying your cat and your house. The only time I recommend using soil in the litter box is when you're re-training an outdoor cat to go indoors. A cat who is used to digging in the backyard garden for his litter box may make a smoother adjustment to indoor living if you fill the box with plain soil. Gradually add clay litter to the box while decreasing the amount of soil as your cat makes the adjustment. Alfalfa pellets can be either good or bad. I've known owners who're tried using the pellets because they're supposed to be so great at controlling odors. Unfortunately, many of the cats hated them and urinated in other places in protest. I have also seen cats who absolutely refused to use clay and accepted the alfalfa pellets without a problem. It's a judgment you have to make based upon what your particular cat prefers.

The Special Case of Declawed Cats

Declawed cats have special needs. If you're having your cat declawed (before taking this permanent step, please read chapter 7 on how to deal with scratching problems) the first two weeks after the operation will be an important time for you to create a comfortable litter box for him. These first ten-fourteen days will also require using the appropriate litter box filler to encourage proper healing. Your vet will probably recommend using shredded newspaper in the box for the first ten days. This is done for two reasons—it's more comfortable on the cat's sensitive paws, and it helps to keep the healing paws clean. Particles in clay or sand litter can get caught in the wounds, causing irritation and possibly infection. I find that cats who are used to regular litter can object to having strips of newspaper in their box. If you consider how stressful the declawing operation is to begin with, you don't want to add a second cause of stress on top of that. Ask your vet about a litter box filler called Yesterday's News. This litter is made from pelletized newspaper. It's comfortable for post-op recovery and has no particles to irritate the paws. I've found that cats adjust better to Yesterday's News litter box filler than regular shredded paper. If you're planning on having your cat declawed, ask your vet to order Yesterday's News in advance so you can start introducing it before the surgery. Planning this beforehand can mean less trauma after the operation.

If you or your cat suffer from an allergy to the dust in regular litter consider using Yesterday's News as your regular litter because it's dust-free.

Some cats' paws remain a little sensitive even long after healing is completed. In this case you might consider using one of the sand-like clumping litters indefinitely. These litter box fillers are much softer on the paws than clay litter.

Emotional/Territorial Causes of Litter Box Rejection

This is a tough problem and unfortunately it's something many owners don't think of. Your cat reacts emotionally to changes in his environment. He can also have difficulty coping with stressful situations. Any upset in your life (marriage, divorce, death in family, job change) is undoubtedly affecting your cat as well. In the case of major traumas such as death or divorce, not only is a cat dealing with his own emotional state, he'll also be picking up on and absorbing your stress. During troubled or stressful times it's easy to neglect the needs of your pets or change the routines they're so used to. This can leave a pet feeling confused and tense.

A major upset that involves the whole household is actually easier to isolate as the cause of behavior problems such as litter box rejection. It's the upset in your cat's life that you aren't aware of that is the toughest to solve. When your normally well-behaved, litter trained kitty starts spraying indoors (and the vet gives a clean bill of health) chances are something is threatening his security and you, his loving owner, must identify the threat and eliminate it.

New House

There are obvious stressful circumstances that can cause a cat to reject his litter box such as a move to a new house. This can be traumatic for a human so imagine how confusing it is to your poor cat. Cats are territorial animals and when you force them to abruptly adjust to unfamiliar surroundings you're asking a lot of them. If you've just moved to a new house or apartment and your cat has stopped using his litter box you've probably overwhelmed him with too much too soon. The best way to avoid potential problems is to not allow your cat to have the run of the entire new house all at once. Setting up a room for him and allowing time for the adjustment will make it much easier. The previous owners of the home might have had animals. Although this house has probably been thoroughly cleaned, those scents are still detectable to your cat's sensitive nose. It may take time before he no longer feels threatened and can begin to establish your home as his own territory.

Abrupt Changes in Food or Litter

Changing a cat's brand of food can be very traumatic to him. The only way he has of protesting is to first stop eating. If you still haven't paid attention, he'll get more dramatic and may leave you an unwelcome present on your carpet. If you're going to switch brands of food do it gradually. Mix a bit of the new food in with the regular food a little at a time so that over the course of a week to ten days you've phased out the old food and painlessly introduced the new kind. All changes should be gradual.

Unfamiliar Faces

New babies, company, new spouses, etc.—these situations can be very threatening to a cat. He may react by rejecting his litter box. If a cat feels his territory is really in danger because of the new addition he may either spray that person's belongings or he may spray your things to make certain everyone knows that you belong to him. He may also go around spraying various pieces of furniture to firmly establish his territory. A cat who is just totally stressed out by all the change and intrusion may start urinating or defecating on the rug or in the tub, eventually rejecting his box completely. He may not be spraying to mark territory but just reacting to an overload of stress and frustration.

To relieve some of the anxiety, allow the cat to get to know the new person so they can develop a bond. In the case of a new baby, let the cat be a part of the whole thing from the very beginning. For specific advice on helping your cat cope with a new baby in the house and the problems that arise, refer to Chapter 12.

If the new addition is an adult such as a spouse, let that person take over the feeding responsibilities. Show your new spouse how to indulge your cat in some favorite games. It's important that your cat not feel his time with you has been cut because of this new stranger so make sure you're lavishing extra attention on him. More on this subject in Chapter 12.

New Furniture/Carpets/Construction

The addition of a carpet with all its unfamiliar smells can cause a cat to feel the need to mark it as his territory. This can happen with just about any piece of furniture. Major renovations or changes in your home can also cause him to get upset or feel threatened. In the case of construction, loud noises such as hammering or drilling, and the intrusion of construction workers going in and out can be very frightening. Keep your cat and his litter box in an undisturbed part of the house during major renovations (it'll also be much safer for him).

If your cat is one who feels threatened by the addition of unfamiliar furniture you may want to cover the new piece or keep your cat away from that room so the furniture can take on some of the familiar scents of the house. The first few times your cat comes in contact with new carpeting or furniture you should supervise.

Multipet Households

To avoid territorial disputes which can lead to litter box rejection, introduce a new pet into the house very carefully. Bringing a second cat into your resident cat's territory can cause all kinds of trouble. The newcomer should have a safe place in a separate room with his own litter box, food bowl, water and toys. Refer to Chapter 11 for instructions on introducing a second pet and for suggested Bach Flower Remedies. The hard part is that you mustn't pay any attention to the newcomer or else your resident cat will feel that not only has his territory been violated but his trusted owner has switched to the enemy's side. Your cat may do a lot of tough posturing and try to intimidate the new guy with hissing, but in time, the two should come to terms and a friendship will develop.

If there's a litter box problem with your cat and you have a newcomer in the house, you'll need to make sure the new guy isn't bulldozing his way through your cat's territory. Two litter boxes may be needed even after the initial introduction period is over. Some cats just totally object to sharing.

If the newcomer is a frisky little puppy, play with the new guy separately to wind him down before bringing him in to meet the cat. This way, the pup won't be so hyper and your cat won't be annoyed. Keep the puppy on a leash if you're unable to control him verbally to prevent him from pouncing relentlessly on your unsuspecting kitty. For more on how to introduce a new puppy to your cat, refer to Chapter 11.

Unfamiliar Faces Outside

Even if you haven't added a second indoor cat to the household it doesn't mean there isn't one outside that your cat knows about. As your sweet little cat is looking out the window he may be seeing a strange cat in the yard across the street or even worse, in your yard. If your cat is an indoor cat then what he may do (since he can't go outside to defend his territory) is to go around the house and spray to mark his turf. In the case of a dog coming in the yard (or it can even be an owner walking his dog along the street every day) your cat may be frightened or tense. This can cause him to reject his litter box. If you notice him at the window right before an episode of indiscriminate urination or spraying then you'd better investigate what's going on outdoors. If it's a cat or dog coming in your yard and you know where he lives, perhaps you can speak to the owner.

If your cat is reacting to any animal that goes by, keep the blinds or curtains drawn on the windows overlooking the trouble spot. When you do this, it helps if you add an indoor distraction for your cat. You could add some extra playtime with you or some new toys. If there's a window overlooking a nice quiet spot in your backyard, set up a little perch there for your cat. If the ledge isn't wide enough you can buy a window shelf made especially for cats. Hobar Manufacturing is one company that makes a good quality shelf that attaches to the window. The shelf is available by mail order. Hobar's address is listed in the Appendix.

Retraining Your Cat

First, don't punish a cat who urinates or defecates outside the litter box. He'll just do it when you're not around or he'll find better hiding spots for taking care of business. Even if you catch the cat in the act, punishment is ineffective. The cat is attracted to a certain spot for a specific reason. If you punish him, it'll just suppress his behavior temporarily. It is extremely important to remember that if stress is playing a key role in your cat's need to urinate outside his box, punishment will only compound the problem. Therefore, never strike or shake your cat, rub his nose in anything he's done, or yell at him.

With a spraying cat, if you actually catch him in the act you can distract him with a loud noise such as a shake can (a few pennies in an empty soda can with the opening taped over). Be aware of the warning signs that the cat is about to spray, such as backing up to an item or tail twitching. But no yelling or punishment. You never want the cat to directly associate the loud noise with you, his loving owner; this only makes him afraid of you. The purpose of the shake can is only to *distract* him. This method must be combined with the proper behavior modification techniques (or else you'll have to follow your cat around the house with your shake can twenty-four hours a day).

What makes one particular item or area a repeat target is the scent. Once a cat urinates on a carpet he'll always be able to detect the scent of his urine in that spot. This is why he returns there to urinate again. Therefore, it's imperative that you not only clean the area but *neutralize* the odor. Just using a rug cleaner or a little soap and water won't do the trick. Even if you can't detect any urine odor, believe me, your cat's sensitive nose will. So before you do anything else, get rid of temptation by neutralizing all odors. Follow the instructions under "Cleaning and Eliminating Stains and Odors" in this chapter.

If your cat is urinating in one or two spots on the floor or carpet there are a couple of tried-and-true methods of retraining. After you've completely cleaned and eliminated the stain and odor, put his food bowl right on that spot at mealtime. Start feeding him in the area he was urinating in because cats don't like to eliminate where they eat. If he's urinating in more than one location, divide his food into several portions and place a bowl at each area. Even after he's eaten the food, leave his bowl there as a reminder that this isn't a rest room. Use this method for a few weeks. Then you can try removing one bowl for a day and then put it back. If all goes well, after a week of removing and replacing the bowl you can take it away completely to see if the cat has permanently been retrained. If he hasn't had any "mistakes" in that spot, after another week you can begin the procedure with the second bowl. Follow this procedure for each bowl and don't be in a rush. You need to make this a slow and gradual change to give him time to get the message. If you rush this method your cat will revert back to the old behavior as soon as the bowls are gone. If that does happen, then begin the whole procedure from the very beginning and this time be a little more patient.

If your cat is urinating in several spots on the carpet get a roll of self-adhesive shelf paper and place pieces of it on the trouble spots (after the area has been odor neutralized). The smooth texture of the shelf paper in many cases discourages the cat. For more stubborn cats, buy a roll of the vinyl carpet runners. Cut the size you need and place that over the spot with the pointed side facing up. Double-sided tape works well too. Some people use waxed paper but it's not nearly as effective and is easy to scratch through. Many people have used foil or even plastic wrap but I don't recommend them because the cat can chew either of those, causing serious intestinal damage. The shelf paper method works well on furniture. If your cat is spraying the back or side of a chair, put the paper over the area. Because of the smoothness of the paper, when he goes to spray there the urine will splatter on him unexpectedly. He won't like that at all. Spray a little citrus scent on the shelf paper to further discourage the cat (they generally dislike the scent). The shelf paper method has the added benefit of preventing any further damage to your carpet or furniture from repeated urination.

Some cats use the bathtub as a litter box. I've known long-haired cats to sometimes do this when their litter box was too dirty. In an effort to keep their long coat clean they'll use the tub. Sometimes cats suffering from cystitis will use the tub instead of their litter box. They may be associating their litter box with the pain they feel. Some cystitis cats may also find comfort in the coolness of the tub's surface. If your cat has chosen the tub, keep about an inch of water in it at all times during the retraining period. Another method that works is to saturate a few cotton balls with a citrus-scented liquid or perfume and place them in a small plastic margarine container with a snap-on lid. Tape the lid onto the container as extra insurance against your cat getting at the cotton balls. Poke a few holes in the lid so the scent comes out. Placing one or two containers in the tub will often deter the cat.

The scented margarine container can also be used to help discourage a cat from repeatedly urinating in a particular spot on an item such as a bedspread. Sometimes it's the *texture* of the material that attracts the cat. In those cases you'd be better off replacing the bedspread with one that has a smoother texture.

Some cats use bath mats as litter box substitutes. They seem to like the texture. Hanging the bath mat up when not in use will solve the problem.

Territorial disputes between roommate cats can account for some litter box problems. In a multicat household you may need to have more than one box. There are also some cats who don't like to defecate in the same box they use for urination. I have several clients who have resolved the problem of their cats messing on the carpet or in the tub just by having two litter boxes set up—one is used exclusively for urinating and the other for solid wastes. It's not as uncommon as you might think.

When Your Cat Uses Your Plants for a Litter Box

There are a few cats who insist on using the soil in the pots of floor plants as their litter box. In many cases the cats who do this are allowed outdoors or were once outdoor cats. They use the soil in the planters because that's what they use outdoors. To solve this problem the first thing to do is completely change the soil in the pots to get rid of the urine odor. If you don't do this then every time you water the plants the odor will come to life again. Next, completely cover the soil in the planters with rocks to discourage the cat (your guests will think you do this to be decorative). Make sure the rocks you use are large enough so your cat can't get into any danger from swallowing them and also so he can't push them out of the pot to get to the soil. You can also lay a little garden netting on the soil.

If your cat is used to eliminating in soil, he may be rejecting his box if you're using clay litter. You can try one of the sand-like litters in case he prefers the softer consistency. After he's using his litter box again, if you want to go back to clay, gradually reintroduce it by mixing a little in with the other litter. Make the changeover slow so your cat won't object. Watch how he reacts to the clay because he may have a very strong preference for the softer litter. If that's the case you'll have to use the sand-like litter exclusively.

For a cat who refuses to use anything but soil, then use that in the litter box with just a little bit of clay or sand-like litter. When your cat is routinely using the box again you can very slowly start increasing the amount of litter while decreasing the amount of soil. For this method to be a success I can't stress enough how gradual the change must be.

Confinement Method for Litter Box Retraining

I use this method when all other possibilities have been exhausted. The reason the confinement method works is that it deals with the cat's instinct not to urinate or defecate in his nest. If you confine him in a small area with his bed and food/water on one side and his litter box on the other, he'll soon learn that he only has one choice.

As for the best place to confine the cat, my choice is the bathroom. It doesn't necessarily have to be the bathroom. You can use any kind of room provided it's small enough to teach the cat that his only choice is to use the box. It must be a room without carpeting, though. You can also use a large cage which will allow your cat to be in the same room with you during the retraining period.

To set up the area, remove all rugs from the bathroom. Put your cat's water bowl and bed on one side and his litter box on the other. During the confinement period the cat will be fed in the bathroom (or cage). Put a couple of toys in the bathroom too, because the purpose is to *retrain* the cat, not to *punish* him. If you're using a cage, make sure it's large enough for your cat to have a comfortable spot between the litter box and the food bowl, and that there's enough room for him to stand up and stretch out.

The cat should be kept in the bathroom or cage for a minimum of five days before being allowed out for periods of freedom. Don't weaken because you feel sorry for the cat and let him out. For the confinement method to work you've got to be consistent. If the cat's confined in the bathroom go in there to pet, groom and play with him often. It's especially important that you maintain your regular grooming and normal feeding schedule. Remember, this is not a punishment, so be loving, positive and attentive. Another important factor in retraining the cat is to *praise* him when he uses his litter box successfully.

After the first five days, only allow the cat out if he has been successfully using his litter box. Sometimes the retraining can take one or two weeks before the cat is faithfully using his litter box. Don't be too quick to let him have his freedom just because he starts to use his box. Make sure he has really become retrained.

If possible, try to be more aware of the time of day your cat usually eliminates. This will be helpful when you begin periods of freedom. When your cat isn't confined you must carefully supervise him until you're sure he's retrained.

When your cat is consistently using his box and you feel confident that he has been retrained, you can discontinue the confinement. When the confinement period is over, though, slowly reintroduce your cat to the house. Don't give him the run of the entire house all at once.

If you have an outdoor cat who is having trouble adjusting to the indoor box, the confinement method will make it easier.

Hormone Therapy for Hard Core Sprayers

A synthetic progesterone (a female hormone) is sometimes prescribed to stop male cats from spraying. Ovaban is the brand name of one such progesterone. Ovaban was originally developed for female dogs to cease their heat cycles. Not approved by the FDA for use in cats, Ovaban is an "extra label" drug, which means it's used for a purpose other than for what it was intended. Veterinarians will sometimes use a drug intended for one species on another when there is no approved drug available.

The use of Ovaban will not eliminate the spraying problem forever because it will return when the drug is discontinued. Also, the use of Ovaban must not be long-term because it can have *serious* health consequences. Cats on Ovaban are at risk for developing diabetes mellitus. If your cat is currently on Ovaban have him tested for diabetes and observe him carefully for the signs associated with the disease (increased water consumption, increased urination, change in weight).

Behavior modification is a much safer and more effective way to treat a cat who sprays. If you and your vet do decide to go ahead with hormone therapy, you must combine it with behavior modification or you'll just see the problem resurface later on.

Ovaban isn't a wonder drug and isn't a treatment to be rushed into. A thorough discussion with your vet is needed. I would be very wary of a vet who immediately prescribed hormone therapy for your cat without first instructing you to try behavior modification or to seek advice from an animal behaviorist.

Eating Litter

This is usually seen in cats suffering from anemia. If your cat is eating litter have the vet do an examination including a blood work-up because an iron supplement may be needed.

Cleaning and Eliminating Stains and Odors

Cleaning Urine from Carpet
- First blot up as much of the urine as you can with paper towels. Be careful not to force the urine down deeper into the carpet.
- After blotting, place dry paper towels over the spot and press down to absorb more liquid. Keep repeating with dry towels until you can't get up any more liquid.

- Next, following label instructions, use a pet stain and odor remover. The best ones contain enzymes that neutralize the odor in urine. If you just use a regular cleaner you'll still have an odor problem (and maybe even a stain problem). Your cat's sensitive nose will be able to pick up the scent of the urine and he'll be attracted right back to the same spot. Never use products containing ammonia to clean urine odor. Urine is partly made up of ammonia and will make your cat think that another cat has urinated there. He'll then need to spray on top of that to reclaim his spot. There are several pet stain and odor removers available. My favorite one is Nature's Miracle. You can find it in your local pet supply store or through mail order catalogs. Not only can it be safely used on carpet, furniture, floors and clothing, but it's totally non-toxic to your pet.
- Be certain to get the enzyme stain and odor remover down deep enough into the carpet. If the urine reached the padding under the carpet be sure it also gets covered with the liquid. Don't rub.
- Leave the enzyme product on the carpet for as long as the label recommends.
- Blot up the liquid with towels until the spot is dry. Don't rub.
- Put a towel down on the spot with something over it for weight. Keep it in place for about an hour or so to absorb the last bit of moisture.

Cleaning Old Urine Stains from Carpet
- First dilute the concentration of urine by applying water to the area. This is an important step in case your cat has urinated on that spot several times. If you don't water it down first there'll be too much ammonia released, which can reduce the digesting power of the enzymes.
- After diluting with water, follow instructions under "Cleaning Urine from Carpet."

Cleaning Feces from Carpet
- Cover your hand with a plastic bag and remove all the solids from the carpet. I find the plastic bag method works better than using paper towels or newspaper because you can see what you're doing. You can't be as accurate with a paper towel or newspaper and can actually make the stain worse.
- Following label instructions, apply the enzyme product and blot until dry as described under "Cleaning Urine from Carpet."
- For diarrhea or very loose stools, I've found the easiest way to pick it up is with a thin metal spatula (I've even used a putty knife). Get up as much of the stool as you can along the top of the carpet

with the putty knife or spatula. Blot up the rest with paper towels and then use the enzyme product. If the diarrhea is so bad that it's purely liquid, don't even use a spatula. Just blot with paper towels and treat it as you would a urine stain.

Cleaning Urine or Feces From Floors
- First blot up the liquid or remove the solids and then apply the enzyme product according to label instructions.
- On non-porous surfaces cleanup is a breeze. Some hard surfaces are porous and some of the urine will have been absorbed. Be sure the enzyme product stays on the surface long enough to penetrate the urine. This will also apply to floors that aren't porous if the urine spot is over a seam or crack.

Emergency Cleanups
I always keep a bottle of Nature's Miracle on hand for any potential accident; it not only works on urine and feces but also on vomit and blood stains. Even if your cat isn't experiencing litter box problems it's a good idea to have the enzyme neutralizer in the house.

In the case of a urine stain catching you unprepared without your trusty enzyme product, the soiled area can be cleaned and deodorized by using a solution of equal parts white vinegar and water.

chapter 7

Scratching Behavior

Those of you who are familiar with my work know how I feel about declawing a cat. Too many people rush out and put their cat through this horrible and unnecessary operation in order to save their furniture. A cat without her front claws is left almost defenseless. Her claws are how she gives warning that we're to back off. When I see an unhappy cat extend her claws I know I've intruded upon her space or upset her somehow. Without the ability to warn with the front claws she has no way to tell you that you've intruded— until you get bitten. I've seen declawed cats become very nervous and resort to biting without giving any warning. Cats without claws are also denied that joyous and natural cat ritual of being able to use a scratching post to unkink muscles and stretch the back.

If you're turning an outdoor cat into an indoor pet and plan to have her declawed, I urge you to think very carefully before having this surgery done. An older cat who has been used to having her claws for climbing and for defense may end up traumatized when she realizes her claws are no longer there. This may lead to the cat becoming a biter.

If you have a kitten, before deciding to have her declawed, please give her a chance to be trained to the proper scratching post and to learn "cat manners" regarding when and where her claws are to be used. Like all children, your kitten needs your loving guidance.

The Problem

Your cat has been scratching the back of your favorite chair. Maybe she's shredding your beautiful living room drapes. You've bought her a scratching post at the pet store but it has been ignored completely. Is your cat being bad and spiteful? No, she's being smart. Your kitty isn't being destructive when she scratches your furniture. Scratching is a natural part of a cat's life and you can either battle with her over this or you can retrain her to scratch where you want her to scratch.

Cats look for appealing scratching surfaces for several reasons. First, it's vital for maintaining physical health by removing the dead outer sheaths to reveal the new claws underneath. If you look at the base of whatever your cat is consistently using as her scratching post you'll see a bunch of those discarded sheaths. I've had concerned owners call me because they've found these nail sheaths at the base of the scratching post or piece of furniture and were worried that the cat's nails had been broken. I've even known of some cases where cat owners have removed the scratching post out of fear that it was actually ruining the cat's claws. Nothing could be further from the truth. These dead nail sheaths must be discarded to maintain healthy claws. If you don't provide a good scratching post, or if your cat can't locate a place to scratch, she may resort to chewing on her claws in an attempt to remove the dead sheaths. This isn't a healthy alternative and can lead to claw and cuticle problems. It is normal, though, for the cat to use her teeth to remove the outer sheaths of the hind claws.

If you only discourage furniture clawing without providing your cat with an allowable scratching surface you'll leave her very frustrated. She may then scratch more often but for shorter periods of time until she gets chased away. She'll also learn to scratch when you're not around. By only using negative behavior training, you may, in addition, be conditioning your cat to be afraid of you.

Another reason for scratching behavior is to stretch and tone the muscles of the shoulders and back. If you've ever seen how tightly curled a cat can sleep for hours you'll appreciate her need for a good stretch afterward. A declawed cat doesn't get to enjoy this luxury.

Scratching behavior can be used for marking territory both visually and with scent (the scent comes from the paw pads). Some cats may scratch near entryways. If your cat is scratching near doors or windows she might be feeling insecure about her territory and the scratching may be more of a behavioral need than a physical need. Treat this as you would a cat who sprays. First, clean the scratched area to eliminate the scent; then cover the spots as described in this chapter under "Training Your Cat to Use the Scratching Post." If your kitty is feeling insecure about her territory you'll need to combine retraining with some detective work to eliminate (or at least modify) the source of her insecurity. Is there a new cat in the neighborhood?

Is there a new person in your house? A new dog? Perhaps you've moved recently (a big source of insecurity for a cat). For a cat unsure about her territory you must include lots of love and attention. Rebuilding her security about her place in the home is vital. A client of mine had a cat who faithfully used her scratching post for years until the family adopted a dog. With the new dog going in and out of the back door so much, Penny started scratching the door frame. Adding a plain wooden scratching post right near the door for her to scratch and mark all she wanted helped Penny adjust to the new family member. With lots of attention and love, she became more comfortable with the dog, and her need to scratch on the wooden post decreased. She soon resumed scratching at her usual post.

Two different kinds of posts may be the answer for you if your cat is scratching near doorways. One post (usually carpeted or sisal covered) will be used for the physical needs and one wooden post will be for the emotional need of marking.

Now, what do you do if your cat isn't using a scratching post at all, but prefers to use your sofa? First, take a look at the kind of material it's made of. Is it a rough material that she can really sink her claws into? Probably. If you have a scratching post in your home that's being ignored, take a look at the kind of material it's made of. Is it made of a rough material that your cat can dig into? Probably not. The post you bought is most likely covered with a fluffy soft carpet. When explaining why a cat chooses to use the furniture to scratch, I tell my clients to think about a nail file. If you needed to file your nails you certainly wouldn't want to use a dull, worn-out file. You'd want to use one that will get the job done efficiently. Your cat is looking for the same thing. When it comes to scratching posts, that fluffy soft one covered with pretty carpet is the feline version of a dull nail file.

Choosing the Right Scratching Post

First, you're going to need to know how to select the right kind of post. The absolute best scratching post I've ever come across is made by the Felix Company. It's a sisal-covered post about 30" high with a strong, heavy base. The post is sturdy and well made. The sisal covering (which has catnip inside for added enticement) is virtually impossible for a cat to resist. The Felix post is available by mail order and is well worth the investment (see the Appendix for their address). If you choose not to get the Felix post then look for one that has a sisal covering or a rough and tough kind of fabric. Don't pick one of those fluffy soft ones or you'll just be wasting your money and dooming your furniture to destruction. The post must also be tall enough to enable your cat to get a good stretch. Even if you find a sisal-covered post, if it's too short your cat will soon outgrow it.

Constructing Your Own Scratching Post

Depending upon how handy you are, constructing your own scratching post can allow you the opportunity to customize it to fit your decor and to accommodate your cat's individual needs. One of the most important aspects of this post will be the choice of covering you pick. Remember the dull versus sharp nail file theory. You'll want to pick a material that will attract your cat exclusively to the post.

Making your own post is especially rewarding if you have a multicat household. One cat may like to scratch on carpet while another may only want to use the sisal-covered post. You can inexpensively please everyone by constructing two or three posts, each covered with a different material.

Because I'm not very handy at all I've made the directions as easy as possible. If you're good at working with your hands and can turn two pieces of wood into a scratching post work-of-art then you'll no doubt put mine to shame. Be creative, keep your cat's needs and personality in mind and you won't go wrong.

Getting Started

Go to your local lumber yard and purchase a 4" x 4" x 30" piece of wood for use as the post. For the base you'll need a 16" x 16" square 3/4" piece of plywood. You can have the salesperson cut the wood to the exact measurements you need (there's sometimes a small charge for this). As for the type of wood to select you can use cedar, redwood, fur or pine. Stay away from very hard woods such as oak because they'll be harder to drill. If you don't plan on covering the base with carpet you'll need to get a piece of sandpaper to smooth it out and eliminate all the rough edges. You might want to sand all the wood a bit even if you're planning on covering everything to avoid splinters while working.

To fasten the post to the base you'll need a screwdriver, a flat-head screw (a 1/4" screw is adequate) and a drill (optional, but it'll make things much easier). Now, if you do have a drill you can use it to put a pilot hole in both the bottom of the post and the base in order to cut down on the amount of work it'll take to get the screw in with the screwdriver. Mark an "x" in the center of the bottom of the post and also one in the center of the base. If you're going to drill a pilot hole be sure it's a smaller size than the screw or else the screw will never hold. For instance, a 1/4" screw should have a 1/8" pilot hole.

If you're going to cover the base with carpeting you'll need to do that before securing the two pieces of wood together. The post itself can be covered before or after you fasten it to the base. I find it easier to cover beforehand.

The Cover Material
As I mentioned earlier, what you use as a covering will determine the success or failure of your post (stability is also of vital importance). Don't rush down to the basement to get that scrap of plush carpet that's been hanging around forever. You'll be making two mistakes: 1. The carpet is probably too soft; 2. If your cat does happen to scratch on it, how is he supposed to differentiate between the carpet on the floor and the carpet around his post? You need to cover the post with a different material so there'll never be any confusion as to what is and isn't allowed.

The leftover piece of carpet you have in the house can still be used on the scratching post with just one minor adjustment. You're going to place the *backside* of the carpet facing out. The rough backing will be very attractive to the cat. If the idea of having to look at the backside of a carpet in your living room doesn't appeal to you then purchase a tightly woven rough carpet (like the indoor/outdoor kind) in a complementary shade to your decor and then you'll be able to use it with the right side facing out. Don't weaken and buy a fluffy soft carpet or your scratching post will just end up being a forgotten dust collector in the corner.

You don't have to be limited to carpet as a cover material for your post. Most cats I know love sisal. One post in my house is covered with a 3/4" rope that was tightly wrapped around. It's a favorite gathering place for my cats. It can be tough trying to guess how much rope to buy for your post so you may want to bring your 4" x 4" wood to the store and take the time to wrap the rope around it to be sure you'll have the correct length. To be safe, get an extra two feet to allow for the fact that you'll be pulling the rope much tighter when you actually get ready to fasten it to the post.

If you're using carpet as a covering you can secure it to the post with carpet tacks along the side seam, top and bottom (before tacking put some catnip inside as a special bonus). If you choose to cover the post with rope you'll need something heavier than carpet tacks as fasteners. We hammered in a heavy staple at the top and bottom of the rope to secure it to the post.

Putting the Two Pieces Together

When it comes time to screw the base and post together, use a flat-head screw. You'll need to countersink the screw so that the base will stand level. Using a flat-head screw makes less work for you. If it's hard getting the screw to go in you can put a little candle wax along the threads. For extra stability use a touch of white glue on the screw.

Another option for securing the post and the base together is to use a hammer and about four 10d (10 penny) nails. If you do use this method, draw an outline of the post square on the base so you'll be certain to avoid placing the nails too close to the edge and causing the wood to splinter. Hammer the nails flush with the base so it'll stand level.

Don't Limit Yourself

While many cats like to scratch on carpet or sisal-covered posts, there are also those who love to scratch on plain wood (as you may already know if your cat is using a doorway or the leg of your dining table). If that's the case, you should leave the post with the plain wood exposed. You can even nail a log into a base of plywood for a more rustic-looking scratching post. Cut the bottom of the log so it stands straight. Depending on how elaborate you want to be you can even create a "cat tree" with a carpeted platform on top of the post for cat naps. Be sure you have a wide, heavy base to ensure stability.

If limited space is a problem try making a scratching pad. Secure the carpet to a flat board and screw it into the wall. The board needs to be the same height as a scratching post so your cat can get a good stretch. A scratching pad is a wonderful idea for narrow hallways or rooms with limited floor space.

Not all cats are vertical scratchers, that is, not all cats want to reach up and scratch. You may find that your kitty prefers to be a horizontal scratcher. Perhaps she is scratching on the welcome mat or on a particular carpet in your home. First, use the self-adhesive shelf paper to cover your carpet and prevent any further damage. Then make a scratching pad (you really need a heavy base for this) that can be left on the floor. You can make it long and narrow to fit along the wall or perfectly square to wedge into a corner. Even if your cat seems to be a horizontal scratcher, it's a good idea to have at least one scratching post for those times when she may prefer vertical scratching.

Training Your Cat to Use the Scratching Post

Under normal circumstances my recommendation would be to put the scratching post near your cat's favorite sleeping place or near the food bowl. After a nap or a meal are two favorite times for a good scratch and stretch. But, if your cat is scratching furniture then we'll need to make a few adjustments before relocating the post to a more permanent place.

Forget about all the previous methods you've used to prevent your cat from scratching furniture. Yelling, spanking, squirting water, etc., are out. The best way to get your cat to stop scratching your furniture is to give her a better place to scratch. She'll think it's her idea and you'll be able to retrain her without much stress to her or to you.

The first step will be to make the furniture no longer appealing as a scratching surface. Get a roll of self-adhesive shelf paper (not Contact paper) and cut a large enough piece to cover the area of the chair or sofa that your cat is scratching. If the chair is being scratched all over you can cover it with a sheet (make sure all corners are tucked in, though, or your cat will just get in underneath and you'll never know how much damage is being done). Now I realize the shelf paper won't look so attractive, but it'll only be temporary—just during the retraining period. You can also use the shelf paper on walls and drapes. I don't advise the use of plastic wrap or aluminum foil because they're too easy for the cat to get off the furniture and they can cause injury should they be ingested. I'm also against taping balloons to the furniture (a method that may have been recommended to you—it's very common). The sudden popping sound of a balloon is much too frightening to put a cat through when there are safer, less stressful (and more successful) methods.

Okay, now that you've made the furniture unappealing you need to place the scratching post close by. This way, when kitty goes over for her usual scratch on the chair she'll see this great new scratching post with that wonderful sisal material. You may need to entice her the first time by dangling a toy (use a feather, the Cat Dancer, or whatever toy is your cat's favorite) over the post. Many times the catnip alone will cause her to check out the post. You can also scratch the post yourself, creating a sound that'll be hard for her to resist. If your cat insists on trying to get to the furniture, bring her over to the post but don't force her to scratch (cats hate to be bossed around). Just run your own nails over the post and act like you're having a great time. It won't take long before she'll join in. Placing the scratching post on its side and having your kitty stand on it can help her if she's still unable to figure out what she's supposed to do. Have a toy nearby and as the two of you play she'll dig her claws into the post and pretty soon she'll forget you're even there. Praise your cat when she gets the idea and starts using the post.

If you've bought the Felix post or made your own wonderful one then it won't take very long to retrain your kitty. Then you'll be able to remove the shelf paper from the furniture. Do this gradually by making the shelf paper smaller and smaller every few days. Don't be in too much of a hurry, though. Wait until you're sure she's consistently going for the post.

Once your cat has been trained you can *gradually* move the post to a permanent location. Don't make the mistake of locating the post in a remote corner of the house or in a room your cat never occupies. Even the best scratching post won't do any good if your cat can't find it. If it's too much trouble to get to the post when your cat has the urge to scratch she'll look for the next best thing. And that could be your favorite chair.

Importance of Pedicures

No scratching post, no matter how wonderful, should ever be viewed as a replacement for trimming your cat's nails. Regularly clipping the tip of the claws will prevent them from getting too long and possibly curling back down into the paw pad. This is very painful and can lead to infection. The other reason for regular nail trimming is that it will lessen any damage done to anything the cat scratches.

Trimming the nails can be done with a trimmer made especially for cats or you can get the kind people use on their own nails. Just don't buy dog nail trimmers because they're too large and you risk cutting off too much of the nail.

To trim, extend the nail by holding the paw in your hand and gently pressing down. Trim just the very tip of the nail. Don't go beyond the curve or you risk clipping the vein where the blood supply is. On light-colored nails you can easily see the pink where the vein starts. With dark nails it'll be harder to trim so always clip less than you think you should. If your cat objects to nail trimming just do one or two at a time. Make it a quick and painless procedure. For a very nervous cat have her get used to you just touching and petting her paws at first. Don't attempt to trim until the cat is comfortable with what you're doing. If you make the process a dreaded painful chore then your cat will surely hide every time she sees the nail trimmers. If you're unsure about how much to trim have your veterinarian give you a demonstration.

chapter 8

Aggression

All aggressive behavior may look the same to you (scratching, biting, hissing, swatting, growling), but the sources can be quite different. There are actually many forms of aggression. Each type of aggression can be quite different. Detecting these differences can help you find and eliminate the true cause of the behavior rather than just blindly trying to temporarily calm an aggressive cat.

The methods you may have used in the past to deal with this behavior, such as yelling, spanking, water pistols, etc., will only heighten the cat's aggression. A cat acts aggressively because he feels threatened. Eliminate (if possible) the threat and then you can calm the cat. No cat is aggressive just to be mean and spiteful. Aggressive behavior causes great stress to a cat so it's not something he's going to take pleasure in.

The types of aggression that are described in this chapter are the more common ones you're likely to run into. Trust me, finding the cause of the aggression is the only way to truly end the behavior.

Territorial Aggression

Cats, unlike dogs, aren't social pack animals. They're territorial beings who come together basically for mating. So whether you have an indoor or outdoor cat, territorial disputes are likely to occur at one time or another when two cats come in contact. Every cat needs to feel he has his own personal territory. You'll find some cats are more adamant about this than others.

Depending upon how dominant he is, an outdoor cat's territory can be confined to his own backyard or can include more of the neighborhood. When dealing with a very territorial cat, you may think you're doing him a favor by letting him outdoors. In fact, you can be causing more stress because you've increased the territory he has to worry about.

With indoor multicat households, territories can be divided up within the home. It can be that one cat rules the upstairs and one rules the lower portion of the house. Territorial divisions can even narrow down to who gets the couch and who gets the chair by the window. The more territory available for each cat the less chance of a dispute. The more cats in one household means a smaller territory for each one. As a result, precious domains may be guarded with tooth and nail.

Time of day can influence territoriality. A cat who claims one particular window or room during the day may not care about it in the evening.

Territorial aggression can be sparked at any time. Life can be going along just fine and then a new cat moves into the neighborhood. Even an indoor cat can feel the threat of a new cat in his backyard. For outdoor cats, if the territorial aggression is being triggered by the appearance of another cat in the neighborhood, there's not much you can do. Neutering your male cat will, in many cases, reduce his inclination to defend his turf so vehemently. If you know where the intruding cat lives, perhaps you can find a way to tactfully speak with his owners about confining their cat. At the very least, find out if the cat has been neutered. If not, the owners should at least agree to that. Your best option in the meantime is to confine your cat indoors (especially if he's coming home with wounds and abscesses). It's not as difficult as you might think, provided you're willing to make a few adjustments. (For more details on that, refer to instructions on changing an outdoor cat into an indoor cat in Chapter 13.)

If your indoor cat is becoming aggressive due to the appearance of another cat (or dog) outside, there are several ways you can help him. As mentioned above, if it's the same cat coming around each time and you know the owners, explain the situation and tell them it's causing a behavior problem with your cat. If that's not possible or if your cat's territorial aggression is triggered by the sight of the next-door neighbor's dog in his own backyard you'll have to work from within. First, if the trouble spot is confined to one window, if possible, close off that room during the key time (usually it's during the day). If it's not an area you can close off then you'll have to keep the curtains or blinds drawn. You may even have to take it another step by blacking out the windows somehow. Perhaps you can install some decorative shutters that he can't poke his head through like he can with curtains. I've had clients install cafe style curtains on the bottom half of the window (use one long cafe curtain so there'll be no opening in the center or sew the two curtains together). Once the curtain is hung fasten each side to the wall or window frame so the cat can't stick his head through.

Whenever you deny a cat access to an "active" window (especially if it used to be his favorite spot before the intruder(s) came along), then you need to create a new favorite spot. Make sure he has access to another good window. If the only safe window looks out on a dull, non-active backyard, then install a bird feeder for him to look out at. Make the new window irresistible. Install a carpeted window shelf for him (Hobar makes a good one—refer to the Appendix). If he has a cat tree, move it near the new window. If he doesn't have a cat tree, consider getting him one. (Cat House Originals lets you design it to fit your taste and budget. Their address is in the Appendix.)

Whenever there's an intruder outside who causes your cat to get agitated and territorial you need to be aware of another form of aggression that can occur; this is called "redirected aggression," and it is discussed in this chapter. It's important that you recognize and know how to handle redirected aggression.

In multicat households, territorial aggression can resurface when a cat returns home after hospitalization or in some cases even after a brief visit to the vet for vaccinations. It may be because the cat no longer smells familiar with those hospital odors. The smells of the hospital may be frightening to the other cat because of the negative association that the veterinarian's office holds for him. If the territorial aggression between your indoor cats is sparked by one cat's return from the vet, first place the returning cat in another room and rub a little brewer's yeast powder into his coat. Also rub some into the coat of the other cat(s). Brewer's yeast is available in natural food stores. I like it because it's all natural, full of vitamin B, and will actually be good for the cats if they lick it off. The smell of the brewer's yeast helps disguise the hospital odors and each cat will basically smell the same. Don't use anything like baby powder because the talc isn't good for the cat to breathe or ingest. Use only brewer's yeast.

Bringing a newcomer into the house almost always brings out the territoriality in the resident cat. Proper introduction of all newcomers (cat, dog, or human) should be done to reduce the chance of aggression and to accelerate acceptance. This is so important that I've dedicated a separate chapter to the subject. Refer to Chapter 11 for the proper introduction of a new companion pet, and Chapter 12 for introducing new family members (new baby, new spouse).

Fear Aggression

When confronted with possible danger, a cat's first reaction is to get away if he can. If escape is out of the question he may crouch down in a corner, paws tucked in, trying to avoid any contact whatsoever. Cats don't roll over in submission to expose a belly the way dogs do.

Another reaction is a combination of "retreat and attack" behavior. This is actually alternating between aggression (swiping with his paw and hissing) and backing off to protect himself. The ears will be pulled down, the coat will be bristled, and the pupils dilated. The arched "Halloween" cat posture is used to make himself appear larger (the cat stands sideways toward the intruder). Kittens often do this when startled by something. For a frightened cat this form of retreat and attack is done with the hope that it'll drive his attacker away. With cats, a lot of posturing is done. Many times a few swipes with the paw is enough to send the troublemaker on his way.

If the attacker still isn't scared off, the frightened cat partially rolls the front part of his body over, turning his head and front paws sideways. The hind legs stay in contact with the ground but the front paws are aimed for swiping. If this aggressive display still doesn't intimidate the attacker then the frightened cat will also include his hind paws in the battle.

An example of fear aggression that you may be all too familiar with is the way your cat acts at the veterinarian's office. It can be like a Jekyll and Hyde personality. If your cat does show fear aggression at the vet, bring him in just for brief petting sessions. This way he won't always associate the trip to the vet with horrible and awful things that have to happen to him there. Call beforehand and check with the receptionist as to when the quietest time would be (hopefully, a morning when no big dogs are scheduled to come in). Praise and reward your cat whenever he responds positively.

Sometimes just the sight of you taking the carrying case out of the closet can set off the aggression because he knows what's coming next. Invest in a carrying case that can be left open and double as a bed.

Line it with a towel and leave it for the cat to use every day as a little retreat. The case will soon begin to lose that horrible association.

If the only time your cat rides in the car is when he's going to the vet then start taking him on short rides (always in his carrier) around the block and back home. Top it off with much praise and a reward. For more on helping a cat adjust to the carrier and trips to the vet, refer to Chapter 16.

An injured cat can become aggressive out of fear. Always approach an injured cat with caution. Use your voice to soothe and reassure him. Putting a towel over the cat's eyes can help calm him while transporting him to the vet. Always be careful when handling an injured cat who shows aggression, even if the cat is your own loving pet. Cat bites can be serious.

Inter-Male Aggression

This is one of the most common forms of aggressive behavior between cats. Inter-male aggression is often done for territorial control; competition (usually over a particular food or just to be "king of the hill"); or when there's a female in estrus nearby, for the right to mate with her.

An unneutered tom develops thick cheek pads and a loose thickness to the skin on the neck. This provides extra protection during fighting in case he's clawed in the face or his opponent gets a grip on his neck. The fights between males are violent and it's very common to see a tom come home with torn ears or abscesses from infected cat bites.

Males become increasingly territorial and aggressive during mating season. Previously established territories are no longer out of bounds as intact males roam in search of a female. When the scent of a female is detected, a violent fight between the males takes place to establish the right to mate with her. Ironically, the female doesn't always allow the victor to mate with her.

The best and only remedy for inter-male aggression is neutering. Neutering your cat will greatly reduce, and in most cases, eliminate fighting between males. Neutering will also eliminate territorial spraying (Chapter 6) in almost all cases. For those instances where a neutered cat continues to fight, the best solution is to make him an indoor cat. For this to be successful you need to make his indoor world interesting so he won't continue to long for outdoor life. Do this by having a good scratching post, rotating toys weekly to prevent boredom, and providing Play Therapy sessions on a regular basis. For more on helping an outdoor cat adjust to indoor life, refer to Chapter 13.

A neutered cat makes a much more even-tempered pet who is no longer under constant stress from increased hormonal levels.

Redirected Aggression

To give you an idea of what redirected aggression is, here's a typical example: Your cat is looking out the window when all of a sudden a strange cat wanders into the yard. Your cat starts growling, and his tail begins to whip back and forth. You go over to try to calm and reassure him and he violently lashes out at you. You, of course, feel confused and hurt. What actually happened was that the aggression your cat felt toward the other cat was redirected toward you because he was in such an emotional state at the moment you touched him.

Redirected aggression can often be misdiagnosed because it seems so unprovoked and can happen without any warning. The sudden attacks are frightening to us and in some cases they are very severe.

The most common cause of redirected aggression is the presence of another cat. This often happens when an indoor cat spots another cat in the yard and is unable to get to the source of his aggression (the intruder) and he becomes highly agitated. Other causes can be visitors in the house, a dog, sudden noises (especially high-pitched), an indoor cat unexpectedly getting caught outdoors, or an indoor/outdoor cat suddenly denied access to the outside.

What makes redirected aggression difficult to pinpoint is that the inaccessible true target of the cat's arousal may have occurred earlier in the day. Your cat can remain in a state of agitation for quite a while. Just because you can't see an immediate cause for your cat's behavior doesn't mean a cat didn't go by the window earlier in the day or a police car with a blaring siren didn't stop on your street in the morning.

The best way to handle a cat in an aroused state is not to handle him at all. Don't try to comfort him because you'll end up getting scratched and/or bitten and your cat will get all the more agitated. Chasing after the cat to calm him, throwing a towel over him, spanking him or grabbing him can actually cause a secondary fear aggression. Don't bother him until you've seen he has gone back to his normal routine (such as eating). And even then, don't try to hold and confine him. It's best to do some easy playtime (such as rolling a ping-pong ball or using the Cat Dancer).

If you know what or who has caused your cat to get so upset, try to remove the source or prevent your cat's exposure (example: close curtains so he can't see the cat outside).

There are times when you might become the target of redirected aggression quite by accident. I'll give you an example: Your cat runs under the bed after being upset by visitors in the house. You innocently walk by the bed and your cat lashes out at your ankle. Your first thought is that your loving, precious cat is becoming unpredictable and mean. When these unprovoked attacks happen repeatedly, some cat owners, at a loss for any explanation why their sweet little pet has become dangerously aggressive, begin to distance themselves emotionally from the cat. Everyone becomes guarded. The relationship between cat and owner deteriorates to a point where the cat may be given away or even euthanized. Before it gets to that point, consider the possibility that the behavior is redirected aggression. With that in mind you can try to track down the original source of the aggression. Keep track of patterns, time of day it happens, where your cat is at the time, etc.

An animal behaviorist can help you if you're unable to make any progress. In the meantime, if you're the target of redirected aggression, don't go after your cat to make up with him or to punish him. Let him calm down. The cat can remain aroused for quite a while after an attack. He may continue to hiss at you for a half hour or so. The cat may even react normally to other members of the family but not to you. Be patient and don't take it personally.

Asocial Aggression

This type of behavior is sometimes seen when an adult cat acts aggressively toward a kitten. A typical example is when a family adopts a kitten for their older cat after the death of his longtime companion. Both the cat and the family are still in mourning but the naturally social kitten doesn't know anything's wrong so she goes right up to the cat and gets a very negative reaction. All the adult cat wants is to be left alone.

When an adult cat's companion dies, don't rush out to adopt a new pet. Your cat is in mourning and is very confused as to why his friend has disappeared. Before introducing another cause of stress (however temporary) into his life by the addition of a strange kitten, boost his spirits and self-confidence. He needs lots and lots of attention and affection. Play Therapy is an absolute must. Of course, the entire family is in mourning and probably doesn't feel much like playing games but your cat needs that security and comfort. This form of communication is the only way you have of letting him know his home is secure, his family is there for him and he's still loved. Use the Bach Flower Remedy Star of Bethlehem (four drops four times a day) during the initial time of distress following the death of a companion. This Remedy is for the sudden emotional shock and to comfort a cat who is unable to accept the much needed security you offer. Then, after the initial shock phase has passed, use the Bach Flower Remedy Honeysuckle for the cat who seems unable to let go of the memories of his former companion and appears lost in the past.

When your cat is over the crisis and is secure in his place in the family again, you can think about whether or not he would benefit from a new companion. The proper introduction of a new friend is crucial to a successful acceptance, though. Refer to Chapter 11 for the correct technique.

Predatory Aggression

The motivation behind this behavior is simply to capture prey. For some humans, this form of feline behavior is the one we find most entertaining and helpful (in the case of rodent control) and yet for others of us, this behavior seems cruel and ruthless (such as in the capture of a baby bird). No matter how you view it, cats are predators and quite excellent ones at that. Even a bell on the collar doesn't always cut down on a cat's success rate. While it may give some prey enough warning to avoid capture, there are more than a few cats who have learned how to get around this handicap and have become incredibly swift. And then again, not all cats are proficient hunters. Some cats show no interest in it at all.

A kitten's hunting skills are sharpened during the lessons his mother provides by bringing live prey back to the nest in order to teach her young students. Kittens also practice on each other through playtime as they pounce and bat at their litter mates' tails and paws.

The Hunt

The cat may begin by walking to a specific area (especially if he's had previous success there). He then begins a low ground search as he walks around the area or he'll sit and wait for signs of movement. When prey is spotted, the cat slinks along at a trot, periodically stopping behind a bush or tree for temporary cover. When he gets close enough to strike, he'll crouch low, eyes never leaving the target. The whiskers spread out, the body is poised and still except for a twitching of the tail in anticipation. When he feels the time is right for the ambush, the cat will raise up his hindquarters and tread with his back feet. Then he springs and pounces.

The Capture

The cat uses an efficient bite to the nape of the neck to kill his prey. The canine teeth, which have special nerves in the base, help direct the cat to the precise spot in order to sever the spinal cord.

Why do some cats continue to pounce on and paw at dead or near-dead prey? There are a few theories on this behavior. One theory is that the cat is still in such an excited state (especially if the capture was difficult) and is releasing tension. Another theory is that a cat who didn't get much training as a kitten in perfecting his neck bite may not yet realize his prey is dead. And some cats may lose interest in an immobilized or dead prey so they attempt to get it to respond again.

What If You Don't Want Your Cat To Hunt?

If you allow your cat outdoors there's very little you can do to stop his inclination to hunt. He's by nature a predator. Feeding him his meal before you let him out may reduce his desire to hunt. A full stomach will also slow him down a bit. As I mentioned before, a bell on his collar may work in some cases. For hunters, it's certainly better to have a bell on the collar than not. For your cat's safety, though, use a breakaway collar in case he gets hung up on a tree branch or caught in a fence.

Don't punish your cat if he brings his captured prey home. He won't connect the punishment with the "crime." If you use punishment he'll still continue to hunt but may become afraid of you. You can't yell at your cat for bringing home a captured mouse and then praise him as you watch him playing with a catnip-filled mouse that you bought. The stalking and pouncing behavior your cat engages in at playtime is the same as his outdoor hunts. Don't confuse him and don't think that by no longer engaging in playtime you'll diminish his desire to hunt. You'll only create boredom when he's inside and he'll want to go out more often.

My best solution is to keep your cat indoors if you don't want him to hunt. You can walk him on a leash if you still want him to enjoy the outdoors (see page 143). If you do decide to confine your cat to the indoors you'll need to make it as interesting and fun as the outdoors. Provide Play Therapy sessions and rotate toys to avoid boredom. For tips on turning an outdoor cat into an indoor one, refer to Chapter 13.

Petting that Leads to Aggression

You're sitting in the chair and your cat jumps up on your lap. Soliciting petting from you, he begins a steady purr. His eyes are closed and he seems very content with the gentle stroking of your hand. Suddenly, he whips his head around, bites you on the hand, and jumps down. You're left completely confused. Why has your loving cat suddenly rejected you and turned into a tiger?

Unfortunately there isn't a definitive answer why a cat suddenly turns hostile under such a peaceful circumstance, but there is a theory that behaviorists seem to agree on. While your cat lounges in your lap, enjoying the gentle stroking, he may begin to doze. Waking suddenly, he may be momentarily confused by his surroundings and the physical contact. The cat may feel threatened sitting in your lap and being "confined" by your hands while in a relaxed state.

Usually, after this short burst of aggression the cat will jump down but only go a short distance. He may even have a confused look on his face. Then, while sitting only a short distance away from you he'll begin to groom himself as if nothing unusual has happened. This is his way of calming himself down and returning to normal.

With very sensitive or nervous cats, petting for too long can be overstimulating, causing him to bite or lash out with a paw. For a cat like this you need to learn his tolerance limit and then never go beyond it. If you've learned from past experience that after ten minutes of petting your cat suddenly lashes out, then stop petting after five minutes and let him spend the remaining time just sitting in your lap. A couple of signs that he's getting close to his threshold are skin twitching or tail flicking.

If your cat likes to sit in your lap but will bite, scratch, or jump down if you so much as pet him one time, then for the time being, be content with the terms he's established. Be patient and you'll gradually be able to increase the contact time. Since you've probably tried to pet him every time he's jumped into your lap you'll need to erase that negative memory for him. Sit on your hands if you have to but refrain from touching him for the first eight or ten times he's in your lap. You want him to feel comfortable, secure, totally free and not threatened in the least. When he appears comfortable enough (don't be discouraged—with some cats it can take months), you can gently place your hand next to him. Do this for the next several times he's in your lap. When he's comfortable with that you can gently pet him one time. Talk soothingly to him and announce your intentions beforehand so you don't startle him. Don't overdo it, just be happy with one stroke. Each time you can increase by one stroke. Always leave him wanting more. If you rush things you'll undo the positive steps made so be conservative.

No matter how relaxed and trusting your cat looks, avoid petting the sensitive stomach area because it'll elicit a defense reaction. This is a natural reaction so don't cause confusion for you or your cat by trying to rub his belly the way you do to your dog.

Aggressive Play

Playtime allows kittens to refine hunting skills. They get to practice the art of stalking, ambushing and capture. A mistake new owners can make with their cute little kitten is to unknowingly train that it's acceptable to bite fingers and hands. I know it's very hard to resist using your ten ready-made "finger toys" when your kitten feels like playing. This may not seem like such a terrible thing when you're dealing with a tiny ten-week-old kitten but as he grows up into a ten pound cat with adult teeth, his playful bites are going to hurt a lot more. If you use your hands as toys and you're a big, rough and tough person your cat won't distinguish between your hand and the delicate hand of your seven-year-old child. So, from the very beginning, teach all family members to be consistent in not allowing the cat to bite. Always use toys when it comes to playtime so your cat can bite and scratch to his heart's content and no one gets hurt.

If your cat does accidentally bite or scratch your hand in play (or if you've been allowing him in the past), don't pull your hand away. To pull away is to react the way prey would and that'll only cause your cat to keep his hold on you. If you look at the way his claws and teeth are shaped you'll see that pulling away will only do more damage to your skin. Your first response should be to push toward your cat. This may sound odd to you but it does work. First, it confuses the cat because he expects you to try to pull away. Also, by pushing toward him you can more easily disengage his claws or teeth. I also add a verbal response whenever a cat bites or scratches. Saying a key word in a higher pitch helps to get the cat's attention. I use a high pitched "ouch" because that's the easiest word to get out when the skin on my hand is getting pierced by sharp teeth. If you use the high-pitched "ouch" every time then eventually when he hears that sound he'll know to release his grip immediately. Once he's learned this trigger word you can use it as he's about to make contact and avoid damage to your skin.

Whenever I'm playing with a cat and he bites me, after disengaging my hand I ignore the cat for a few minutes. I don't hit or scream at him, I just ignore him. This sends the message to him that whenever he bites or scratches somebody's hand, playtime ends. After a few minutes I'll get a toy and resume playtime. This will show him what is acceptable to bite. After all, you don't want to send the message to him that biting/scratching is totally forbidden. You want to send the message that biting/scratching is forbidden on humans. Never hit a cat for biting you. Never hit a cat for anything. All you'll accomplish is to make the cat afraid of you. Then when you go to pet him he won't know if he's going to get hit or not. He'll either run from you or assume a defensive posture.

A common complaint I hear from owners is that their cat will unexpectedly ambush them (usually attacking ankles) when they walk by a bed that the cat is underneath. One way to stop this is to provide more playtime using interactive toys. Schedule daily playtime (at least two or three fifteen-minute sessions daily) to help alleviate your cat's pent up energy. He won't need to attack your ankles if you're providing enough playtime for him. Also, if you're gone during the day, rotate toys every few days to avoid boredom.

The Importance of Toys

As you know by now, toys are essential when it comes to saving your fingers and hands. For cats who play enthusiastically you'll want to use toys that'll put a safe distance between his teeth/claws and your fingers. Toys like the Cat Dancer, the Kitty Tease or a peacock feather will be your best choices. You can be just as involved in the playtime this way and not get injured. If you've been holding a four-inch catnip mouse between your fingers during playtime you can't expect an excited cat to always be cautious enough to avoid nailing a finger or two by accident. If your cat gets completely carried away during play, then make it easy on everyone and use an interactive toy. You can still keep smaller toys around for him to play with on his own. The interactive fishing pole-type toys will be the special ones you use together.

Food Aggression

This type of aggression is much more common among dogs but there are a few cats who get possessive over their dinner. The behavior you'll see is crouching low over the bowl, usually accompanied by growling.

Manipulation of the diet can help this aggression. Feed more frequent smaller meals. If you've been feeding your cat once a day switch to two or three smaller meals. Don't increase the amount of food you're feeding, just divide the portions. In extreme food aggression cases, leave dry food available free choice to ease the cat's anxiety over the limited availability of food. Watch your cat's weight, though, because you don't want to add the additional problem of obesity.

Dry food has less of an aroma than canned food so you can include more dry in the diet. Be sure it's a top quality, low magnesium dry food to reduce the risk of lower urinary tract disease.

In multicat households some competitive eating may be going on by the more dominant cat of the group. If necessary, distance the cats during mealtimes to alleviate this and relieve anxiety. In some cases you may need to feed in separate rooms. Feed each cat's dinner in his own bowl and serve meals in the same location every time. Don't allow one cat to steal from another cat's bowl. Teach all cats that they're to eat only from their own bowls and you'll eventually relieve mealtime anxiety. It may mean that for a while you'll have to stand guard in the kitchen, but it's important that everyone feel secure during meals. Training your cats now to their own food bowls will be beneficial as they age in case one develops a medical condition requiring a special diet. If they know not to steal from another's bowl, you'll be able to monitor each cat's food intake and feed specific diets as needed.

Pain-Induced Aggression

Pain triggers an aggressive response in most animals. If you have ever spanked your cat you've probably received a paw swipe in return. That's why you don't want to ever punish your cat by hitting him. Spanking also makes the cat afraid of you. He may tense up or run whenever you go to pet him if he associates your hands with pain and punishment. Hopefully, by reading this book you're already aware that behavior modification is the best way to change the undesirable actions of your cat.

During grooming is often the time owners experience pain-induced aggression. For long-haired cats where matting occurs this is an especially important issue. Don't make grooming a torture session for your cat. I tell owners that if the cat hates being groomed then they're doing it wrong. For long-haired cats, do a little every day (literally just a few minutes) to keep the coat free of mats. Also, this way you won't be testing the limits of your cat's patience. Short-haired cats can be groomed two or three times a week.

Be relaxed when you groom. Put on your favorite music (cats respond well to classical). Talk to your cat during the session to constantly reassure him. Use the proper tools for your cat's coat. For short-haired cats use the small, gentle Slicker brush. First, finger comb to find any bumps or wounds on your cat's body. Then when you start to brush use light and short strokes. If you do it correctly it should feel like a massage. To get an idea of how lightly to stroke you can run the brush along your own arm. For long-haired cats, have a variety of combs (wide tooth, medium and fine). First, finger comb your cat to identify any problem areas such as wounds, bumps or mats. Pulling the mats usually causes the pain-induced aggression. Split the mat into small sections by using round tip scissors. A cat's skin is very loose and can easily be mistaken for hair so be very careful. Slide a comb between the mat and the skin (or place your fingers there) to avoid cutting the skin. Face the round tip scissors toward the skin. Don't pull on the mat as you snip or you'll be pulling the skin. Give frequent breaks so your cat doesn't learn to hate this. For cats with several mats (especially in sensitive areas like the stomach, armpits, or around the rear) a professional groomer is your best bet.

Nail trimming is another common pain-induced aggression trigger. Use nail trimmers meant for cats or use regular nail trimmers meant for people. Trim only the very tip before the curve of the nail or else you'll cut the "quick" where the blood supply starts and you'll cause pain. For cats who hate having their paws touched don't try to do all the nails at once. Do one or two a day. Once the nails are trimmed they'll only have to be done every few weeks or so depending on how fast they grow. If you've never trimmed a cat's nails before have a groomer or your veterinarian show you how.

If your cat has a negative association with grooming because of past experience, start from the beginning. Reintroduce him to the joy and pleasure of it by doing his favorite things first. If he likes to be brushed under his chin do that first and repeat it every now and then to keep him happy. If you do something to accidentally hurt him then stop immediately. Do everything you can to make grooming a pleasurable experience and you'll both breeze through it. Remember to give lots of praise afterward and finish with a nice treat like a brewer's yeast tablet or a little yogurt.

For serious pain-induced aggression from such traumatic experiences as being hit by a car, animal attacks, emotional shock, etc., the Bach Flower Remedies can be a big help to calm and comfort. For aggression caused by painful medical conditions (periodontal disease, abscesses, LUTD, etc.) refer to the section "Medically Related Aggression" that follows.

Medically Related Aggression

Your cat has become moody for no apparent reason. Perhaps your loving, affectionate kitty suddenly becomes a vicious tiger whenever petted or held. This unexpected aggressive behavior could be medically related.

Abscesses

Abscesses are often the cause of sudden and severe aggression whenever the cat is touched. If your cat is allowed outdoors and he gets into a fight with another cat (or if your indoor cat fights with a companion cat) he may come back seemingly unharmed. But he may have received a bite or been scratched by his opponent. You may not be able to detect any wound at all but the tiny puncture can seal over, trapping bacteria underneath. Puncture wounds are the most common kind that cats get. These wounds don't bleed much and because of all the fur they are very difficult to see—until the abscess forms. The accumulation of pus and fluid forms a soft lump just under the skin. This is very painful to the touch (very often there can be an accompanying fever). So when you innocently go to stroke your cat you may hit this spot, sending him into a state of both pain and confusion. If you do detect an abscess, get your cat to the veterinarian right away—the sooner the better. If the abscess doesn't burst open on its own (with the help of your cat's tongue), the vet will have to lance it, allow it to drain, and instruct you on treating the area to prevent the wound from sealing over again. For large abscesses, the cat may have to be anesthetized while a drainage tube is stitched in to allow the area to drain over several days.

Tooth and Gum Problems

An abscess isn't the only medical condition that can cause a cat to lash out. Tooth pain and gum disease can also bring out aggression. A broken tooth or swollen, sensitive gums can not only cause pain for a cat trying to eat, they can cause him to become moody and aggressive if you go to scratch him under the chin. If the gum disease has advanced enough, the cat's entire body can feel out of sorts.

Some signs that your cat may have dental problems are bad breath; inflamed, swollen or bleeding gums; tartar-coated teeth; drooling; pawing at mouth; or trouble eating (you may notice a weight loss).

Gingivitis and periodontal disease are serious, so check your cat's mouth routinely and brush his teeth daily if possible, but at least three times a week, with a toothpaste made for cats. Don't use human toothpaste because it can damage the esophagus and stomach.

Accustom your cat to having his teeth brushed by gradually getting him comfortable with each step. For the first few days just pet him around the mouth. Then, when he's comfortable with that, slide your finger inside and gently rub along the teeth. Do this every day.

The next step is to put some toothpaste on your finger and rub along the teeth. Gradually work up to being able to use a gauze pad or toothbrush with a little toothpaste on it. Some cats will never tolerate a toothbrush so if you've tried and tried, use whatever he'll accept. It may always have to be just a little gauze pad wrapped around your finger. After brushing, you don't have to rinse your cat's teeth. Just give lots of praise and love. If you have questions about dental care for cats or how to properly brush the teeth, ask your vet. Sometimes a professional cleaning needs to be done. Under anesthesia, an ultrasonic scaler is used and then the teeth are polished. Don't neglect your cat's teeth because serious periodontal disease can develop.

Lower Urinary Tract Disease

Sometimes referred to as cystitis or FUS (feline urologic syndrome), LUTD is a condition where crystals form in the urine, causing irritation to the bladder and urethra. Diet plays a major role in helping to avoid this painful condition. Foods high in magnesium (magnesium is one of the minerals that make up "ash") contribute to the formation of these crystals. The irritating crystals in the bladder and urethra cause pain, swelling, burning and eventually bleeding. Urination becomes painful and in more advanced cases, impossible, as the crystals block the urethra.

LUTD is a very serious condition and isn't limited to male cats. Some symptoms of LUTD are frequent trips to the litter box, voiding small amounts of urine, random wetting outside of the box, straining or crying during urination attempts, frequent licking of the genital area, and blood in the urine. Don't assume your cat is just constipated if you see him straining in the litter box. Get to your veterinarian immediately.

Cats suffering from LUTD can appear to be restless. Some owners may notice that the cat appears depressed. Loss of appetite is common. The time a cat may become aggressive is when the owner tries handling him too much. During recovery from LUTD provide your cat with lots of support but don't pick him up too much as he's undoubtedly very uncomfortable. Generally, cats with LUTD like warm and cozy spots to sleep—like a chair near a sunny window or close to the heating vent. Some cats, though, prefer cool areas like the bathtub or tiled kitchen floor. Make sure your cat has a comfortable bed for himself away from household traffic.

To hopefully avoid LUTD in the first place or for cats who have had it in the past, make sure you're feeding a high quality, low magnesium food. Keeping the urine acidic to dissolve crystals is important. For LUTD-prone cats your vet will prescribe a specific food. It's imperative that you comply with his or her instructions and not sneak treat goods (such as table scraps or supermarket "gourmet" cat food) to your cat. Once a cat has had LUTD he's likely to get it again if dietary changes aren't made.

For more on litter box problems associated with LUTD, refer to Chapter 6.

Liver Disease

The liver, one of the body's largest organs, serves many functions. Some of them include detoxifying poisons (such as chemicals), manufacturing certain hormones, detoxifying excess amounts of hormones, and producing bile for digestion of fats. A cat's behavior can be adversely affected with an ill temper, for example, if the hormones do become unbalanced.

Some symptoms of liver disease include vomiting, diarrhea, weight loss, dehydration, and fever. Many of the symptoms can also be associated with other diseases, so your vet will need to do a blood test.

To help with temperamental behavior in cats with liver disease, follow your veterinarian's dietary recommendations. Ask him or her about including vitamin C and vitamin B in the diet to help with stress. Protect the cat from toxins such as exposure to household chemicals, paint fumes, foods with preservatives (such as BHA and BHT), insecticides, mothball fumes (very deadly).

Hypothyroidism/Hyperthyroidism

Thyroxin, the hormone produced by the thyroid gland, regulates metabolism. Hypothyroidism means not enough thyroxin is being produced and the body's metabolism slows down. The opposite condition is called hyperthyroidism.

Hypothyroid cats become sluggish, preferring to curl up in a sunny spot and sleep. Most of the time the cat will just appear unenthusiastic but he can become irritable and testy. Some symptoms of hypothyroidism include lethargy, irritability, weight gain (although appetite may appear poor), and greasy coat.

Hyperthyroid cats can be testy and high-strung. Your veterinarian can do a thyroid profile blood test to determine hypothyroidism or hyperthyroidism.

Kidney Disease

The kidneys' job is to filter wastes and toxins from the blood. As with other medically related aggressive episodes, the cat is irritable basically because he doesn't feel well. Early diagnosis of medical conditions such as kidney disease is vital for successful treatment.

Symptoms of kidney disease can include lethargy, vomiting, poor appetite, bad odor from mouth, increased water consumption, increased urination, greasy coat, dandruff, and blood in the urine.

It's important that you work closely with your veterinarian in terms of treatment and dietary management. To ease the kidneys' work load, a reduced protein diet will be necessary (but the protein must be of high quality). Your vet will prescribe the specific diet (such as Hill's k/d).

In addition to specific dietary changes you'll be making, don't overlook the water your cat drinks. Switch to spring water to ensure purity and eliminate metals and excess minerals.

Long-Term Illnesses

To help with irritability, depression, aggression, and other emotional imbalances that often accompany long-term illness, the Bach Flower Remedies can be very helpful. Find the ones that best fit your individual cat and try to use a maximum of four remedies. By becoming familiar with all 38 of the remedies you may find one not mentioned in this book that better suits your cat. I urge you to learn more about the Bach Flower Remedies and how they can help your cat during stressful times.

Learned Aggression

This results from a cat's response to a threat that gets the effect he wants. Example: Your cat is chased by a child. He gets cornered and to defend himself he swipes at the attacker. His claws make contact and the child runs away. The cat may then feel that all children should be dealt with that way. So whenever he encounters a child, instead of retreating he may go on the offensive each time. After being the target of a child's unwelcome grabbing or hitting, the cat may learn that a paw swipe always causes the child to back off.

Physical punishment to the cat in this case, as in all cases, will only make things worse: it will make him more afraid or even more aggressive.

Teach children how to approach and pet (open-handed petting) a cat. Never let a child tease a cat and teach the child to respect the cat's need for space (meaning a sleeping or eating cat is off limits, as is a cat engaged in watching birds outside the window).

If dogs or other cats are the cause of your outdoor cat's learned aggression, keep him indoors. (See Chapter 13 on how to turn him into an indoor cat.) If your cat's learned aggression is directed toward your own dog then follow the instructions in Chapter 11. That method can be used to reintroduce the dog to the cat and help him begin to erase those negative memories. With a cat who already has had a very negative reaction to a dog in the past, you must proceed *very* slowly and don't continue if you feel you can't trust your dog or cat.

It isn't worth anyone getting injured. In this case you'll be better off consulting a professional dog trainer or animal behaviorist.

Maternal Aggression

Most female cats are comfortable enough with their owners to allow them to be a part of raising her kittens. Just make sure she has a safe spot to use as her nest. If the nest is too close to all the household traffic or if you're not allowing her enough private time with her family, she'll move her kittens to a more secluded spot.

With an extremely aggressive mother, refrain from handling the kittens while she's around. When she goes off to use the litter box or to eat you can begin to pet and hold her kittens briefly. Don't allow her to feel threatened and she'll gradually become more comfortable with your presence around her kittens.

Human contact is extremely important in raising a well-socialized, friendly kitten, so try to get them comfortable with your touch and the touch of other family members. Don't intrude on their mealtime or sleep time and never upset the mother. When she's around use a soothing tone of voice. It doesn't hurt to bring her a little of her favorite food either. Don't make her defensive by trying to hand her the food, just leave it nearby as a gift from her loving owner. Set up an ionizer in the same room with her (see page 102).

Aggression Caused by Improper Handling

You can't really blame a cat for voicing his objections if he's restrained against his will, clutched too tightly, or otherwise held improperly.

Respect your cat's feelings and when you hold him, consider his comfort and security. Teach your children how and when to pet the cat with gentle, open-handed petting. Demonstrate how to hold a cat in your arms and explain to your children that a cat is a living creature, not a toy that can be held any which way. Too often, I've seen children clutching a cat in such a way that they appear to be dragging the poor creature.

Don't try to hold a cat who's struggling to get away. Not every cat wants to be a lap cat. The more you insist on keeping the cat on your lap, the less likely he'll ever want to be there again.

The Right Way to Pick Up a Cat
It may seem silly to you that one would need directions on how to do something like bending down to pick up an eight-pound animal. How-

ever, I feel this little act of picking up a cat is too often taken for granted and is where the trouble begins for all the owners who have never been able to hold their cats. I can't tell you how many owners complain to me that their cats hate being held. It doesn't have to be that way but in order for things to change you have to be patient and follow these directions.

First, never just come up behind your cat and startle him by grabbing. This isn't a very nice way to awaken a sleeping kitty. Also, if your cat is engrossed in watching another cat outside the window, your sudden movement can startle him enough that in his excited state he could lash out at you. So always make your presence known before you do anything. For nervous cats this is vital. How you'll announce yourself is by speaking (use a soothing tone) and coming into your cat's field of vision. Then, take a minute to pet your kitty.

No matter how big or little your cat is, *never* pick him up with one hand. I hate seeing cats being hauled around held only by their midriff. It's more difficult for them to breathe and it's very uncomfortable. The right way to pick a cat up is to first face him away from you then slip one hand under his hindquarters and the other hand under his chest. The cat can then rest his forepaws on your arm for support but he won't feel like he's being restrained.

For the cat who isn't comfortable being held for any length of time, practice just picking him up and placing him right back down again. Do this several times a day. After a few days you'll find him getting more at ease. For a very nervous cat you may only be able to pick him up a few inches off the ground before placing him back down. You might have to first spend lots of little sessions with him getting used to having you close by. Always reassure him with your voice. Don't be discouraged if it takes weeks of just picking him up and placing him right back down before he feels comfortable. Better to invest three weeks for a lifetime of cooperation than to rush it and always have a struggling cat. Don't forget to praise him every time. Gradually increase the length of time you hold him and don't be in a rush to hold him longer than he wants. Always place him back on the floor before he starts to struggle. Never let him just jump out of your arms. Always place him gently back on the floor—don't just drop him. Don't do these practice sessions at times when he's busy looking out a window, sleeping, eating, or in his favorite spot. You don't want him thinking that you're always taking him away from his favorite places.

When your cat accepts being held you can practice walking from one spot to another with him in your arms. Always leave him back where you started and have a treat for him (a healthy one like a brewer's yeast tablet). Don't forget lots of praise!

Aggression for Seemingly No Reason

Before you assume your cat is being aggressive for no apparent reason make sure you've ruled out the other possibilities. First, have your cat checked by the vet to rule out any underlying medical cause. Next, look around the cat's environment to detect any possible cause of stress (recent visitors, new baby, other pets, changes in your work hours, strange cats outside, etc.).

Many times with cases like this I find the cat has so much energy that doesn't get expelled in a nice even manner. Eventually the cat gets bored and irritable. When the cat shows some aggressive behavior (such as attacking your ankles as you walk by), the owner gets confused and the bond between them starts to disintegrate.

Provide a regular schedule of playtime between you and your cat using interactive toys. The cat, who is such an incredible hunter, requires stimulation. Those furry mice you toss on the floor are the equivalent of dead prey; they provide no challenge. Regular playtime with you (as well as solitary playtime) is essential for a cat's emotional and physical health. Believe me, something as simple as that can change a cat's disposition. And don't tell me your cat doesn't like to play. Every cat will play provided you find the right toy (and that doesn't mean you have to spend a lot of money on the toy). If you work long hours and your cat is suffering from boredom you may want to consider adopting a companion cat.

chapter 9

Stress and Nervousness

Cats can suffer from stress in the same way that people do. While we're probably aware of the major traumatic events that can stress our cats (such as injury, illness, being lost outside, etc.), we often overlook some everyday causes of stress. When dealing with a cat you have to look at the world through her eyes. The most important factor to keep in mind while viewing your kitty's surroundings as she does, is that cats are creatures of habit. There's a great deal of security in ritual. Take a comforting, daily routine and change it just a little and you can cause a cat stress and worry. Humans love variety and we try every new thing that comes along. Cats take great comfort in familiarity. Take for example the litter box. While at the supermarket one day you see a new brand of litter and it costs less than the usual kind you buy. So you bring it home and fill the box. Your unsuspecting cat casually saunters over and hops into her box expecting to find the litter she's used to. Then suddenly her nose picks up an unfamiliar scent. The pads of her feet tell her the texture of this litter is all wrong. While many cats will make the adjustment without much concern, there are some who'll be confused and unhappy with the change. In some cases, rather than use the unfamiliar litter, the cat will go outside of the litter box. This kind of stressful reaction can happen in other situations, not just with the litter; it can happen whenever abrupt changes are made. Remember this whenever you're going to make any kind of change in your cat's life—from changing food to redecorating your home. Do everything gradually.

While it's virtually impossible to eliminate all causes of stress, we can at least reduce as many of the potentially stressful conditions as are in our control. By being aware of the fact that our cat's threshold for stress is a great deal lower than our own, we can anticipate potential problems earlier and help ease our little companion through necessary changes in a kinder way.

You can turn a healthy, calm cat into a nervous one if she's exposed to stress for too long a time. Symptoms of a nervous cat can include trembling, hiding, hissing, and fear of being held.

Nervousness can be caused by any number of things. The only way to solve the problem is to uncover the cause and, if possible, eliminate it or at least modify it as much as possible. The first step is to have your cat get a thorough examination by the veterinarian because the nervousness may be caused by pain or discomfort. Sometimes it can even be something totally unexpected (such as deafness that had been previously undetected). Once the vet has ruled out any medical cause you can go back home to begin your investigation. You'll need to go through your home to identify possible causes of stress. To help you, I've listed some possibilities.

- A too dirty litter box can stress a cat. If left dirty on a regular basis, it can turn her into a nervous kitty. Remember that predators are attracted to the cat's nest by scent, so as far as your cat is concerned her home is no longer safe.
- Changes in litter brands or location of the box can be stressful.
- Don't place food bowl close to the litter box (cats don't eliminate where they eat).
- Loud noises can be very frightening. This doesn't necessarily mean unusually loud noises either. Shouting, sudden slamming of doors, loud music, baby cries, children screaming, etc., can make some cats nervous. Vacuum cleaners, garbage disposals, and other noisy household appliances are often the cause of nervousness.
- Watch how your children handle the cat. Rough play, improper handling, teasing, or disturbing a sleeping cat can send her into hiding. Teach children how to handle the kitty and to respect her

privacy. Your cat needs to have a safe place to get away from children if she chooses.

- Watch how your cat acts around visitors. Instruct guests to respect your cat's need for privacy.
- Check out the view from windows to determine if your cat's nervousness is due to feline or canine intruders in the yard (if so, refer to "Territorial Aggression").
- Changes in environment are extremely stressful. Moving to a new home, marriage, divorce, new baby, even rearranging furniture, or installing a new carpet can be tough on a cat. Help her adjust by making any disruption in her life as gradual as you can.
- New pets in the house are especially stressful. Refer to Chapter 11 for how to introduce a second pet.
- Avoid abrupt changes in food. Gradually mix a small amount of the new food into the regular brand. This will also help avoid intestinal upsets.
- If you travel and are having a sitter come in to care for your cat, instruct him or her on your cat's normal routine and how to do Play Therapy with her. Having a stranger come in and care for your cat in an entirely different way than she's used to can be very stressful.
- Placing your cat in a boarding facility while you're out of town can be extremely stressful, and in some cases, traumatic for her.
- The death or disappearance of a companion animal can be confusing and stressful to your cat.
- Nervousness can be the result of past experiences such as abuse, an outdoor cat not used to indoor noises, a previous household that was very noisy, accidents, etc.

The examples listed above are just a few of the more common causes of nervousness. Since every cat has her own individual personality, don't limit yourself to this list when trying to reduce your kitty's stress. It may not be just one thing that's causing the problem, but a combination of things.

Helping a Nervous Kitty

In general, helping to build your cat's self-confidence and creating a more comforting environment will help her cope with whatever is the cause of her worry.

The Environment
Cats respond positively to classical music. Playing some soothing classical pieces may provide some comfort. Choose music that doesn't

have sharp contrasts in dynamics. Piano or violin concertos are a better choice than highly dynamic symphonies. If you're not a classical music fan perhaps some New Age music would serve as a compromise between pop and classical. Many New Age pieces have beautiful melodies in an atmosphere of peace and tranquillity. I often use New Age music during therapy sessions with aggressive or nervous cats. There's a wide variety of music available, ranging from sounds of nature to beautiful piano pieces. Play the music at a low volume (remember, cats have very sensitive hearing). Another way to provide a more comforting environment is to make sure your cat has a few cozy places for napping or hiding. Perhaps it can be a favorite chair near a sunny window for sleeping or curled up in a corner of the closet in the guest bedroom (with the door always left open of course). A cat with a low stress tolerance needs a few hiding places and peaceful retreats.

Generally, cats feel more secure in elevated places or in hidden spots. Allow your cat a few elevated retreats so she can get away from other people or pets (such as a dog annoying her when she wants to sleep or children attempting to coax her into play).

In terms of areas on the floor, provide a nervous cat with a special bed that allows her the security of not being seen. Unlike dogs, many cats aren't too interested in the typical open-style pet bed. If a cat is going to sleep on ground level she will want to feel a little more protected. Look for a bed that's designed for making a cat feel secure. An A-frame style bed is a great design and creates a hiding place, yet a cat can peek out at the world. It measures approximately 21 inches tall and 20 inches in diameter at the base. This popular bed is available at many pet supply stores or through mail order catalogs. If you have

trouble locating an A-frame bed you can order it through mail order catalogs. Refer to the Appendix for addresses.

The ultimate in hiding places is a cat tree. There are many brands and styles available. Look for a sturdy one with a couple of strong perches on top. If you'd like to design your own, you can contact Cat House Originals and they'll construct it to your specifications using a variety of components (perches, tunnels, houses) and a choice of colors. The cost depends on how elaborate you want your tree to be. They come fully assembled and don't require the use of a ceiling tension pole for security. I've had one in my house for years and it's not only the most popular spot for my cats, it's always a conversation piece with new guests. Our cat tree was a blessing of security for my cats when a new puppy entered our lives. Refer to the Appendix for the address of Cat House Originals.

To provide a nervous cat with a cozy hiding place doesn't have to require spending money. Just turning a box on its side and lining it with a towel might be all the privacy your cat requires. Use your imagination and I'll bet you'll come up with some wonderful ways to give your cat a more secure environment.

Ionizers

Ionizers send out a constant supply of negative ions. These negative ions are usually in abundance in sunshine, at the beach, in water sprays. I'm sure you've noticed how much more peaceful you feel near the shore or on a sunny day. It's the negative ions that are at work. Positive ions in the air tend to make you feel more depressed. Cigarette smoke, pollution and dust can cause too many positive ions to be in the environment. That's where the ionizer can establish the right balance and send out all those wonderful little negative ions to lift your cat's spirits.

When shopping for an ionizer, choose one that *filters* the air as it sends out negative ions. This machine is great for cats suffering from asthma or other respiratory ailments. If you're allergic to cats the ionizer will be filtering the air so you'll notice that breathing will be easier. Ionizers are available in many stores and catalogs. The brand I like the best is made by the Neo-Life Company. You can contact them for the name of a distributor in your area. Neo-Life's address is listed in the Appendix.

Building Your Cat's Self-Confidence

If you've been able to identify and hopefully eliminate the cause of your cat's stress, you're already on the road to encouraging a more confident kitty.

Now that the environment is more comforting you need to devote

time to increasing your cat's sense of security and helping her redis-
cover the joys in her life. One of the best ways to do this is with
playtime. I know you're probably thinking that your cat doesn't like to
play because she's so frightened or nervous all of the time. Well,
playtime is exactly what she needs to release all that nervous tension
and distract her from her worries. If done correctly, playtime is really
a form of therapy for cats. Play Therapy involves using the right toys
in the right way at the right time. Don't run out and buy a bunch of
toys and expect your cat to know what to do with them, especially if
it's been a long time since she's played. This has to be carefully planned
out. Refer to Chapter 4 on Play Therapy.

Vitamin Support for Stress

Vitamin C
The body's requirement for this vitamin is increased during times of
stress (and any behavioral change your cat is going through is stressful for her). Vitamin C is water soluble and isn't stored by the body.
Excess amounts of vitamin C are excreted in the urine. An additional
benefit of supplementing with vitamin C as needed is that it may help
to acidify the urine (acidic urine dissolves the crystals which cause
lower urinary tract disease).

Give a *crushed* 100mg tablet mixed in the food once daily during
highly stressful times. Be sure it's crushed and always mix it in canned
food. Because it's an acidic vitamin you want it to go smoothly into
the stomach or you risk irritating your kitty's esophagus. If you feed
canned food exclusively you can split the dosage (50mg in the morning meal and 50mg in the evening). Don't give anything higher than a
100mg tablet because it will mostly be excreted in the urine. Supplement with vitamin C about three times a week during moderately
stressful times. In crisis situations you can supplement daily until the
initial trauma is over. Then supplement two-three times a week.

Vitamin B Complex
This is another water soluble vitamin that is not stored by the body
and is used in times of stress. Vitamin B helps to calm a kitty during
undesirable behavior periods and also when a cat's normal routine is
interrupted (such as moving, visitors, vet visits, etc.).

When shopping for vitamin B, always get the B complex so you'll
be sure to get the all-important B-6 and pantothenic acid.

The dosage should be 10-15mg daily. *Crush* the tablet and mix it
in some canned food. If you feed canned food twice a day you can
divide 5-7 1/2mg in the morning meal and 5-7 1/2mg in the evening

meal. Supplement three times a week. As with vitamin C, you can supplement daily during a crisis situation, then taper off to two-three times a week. When things are calm again and your cat is back to her old self you no longer have to supplement with vitamin B on a regular basis.

chapter 10

Depression

Do cats get depressed? Are cats actually capable of experiencing such an emotion or are we just attaching human feelings to an animal's behavior? There are many people who don't believe cats are able to experience depression. Those of us who have relationships with cats know that such sensitive and intelligent creatures are capable of many emotions. Depression is just one of those emotions.

If you suspect that your cat is depressed, the first step is to visit the veterinarian. There could be a medical reason for the change in behavior.

What causes depression in a cat? Actually, the very things that can cause a person to become depressed can also affect a cat. For example, any family crisis, such as the death of a family member or a companion pet, divorce, or even a child going off to college can all bring about depression in a cat. When there's a crisis situation such as a death or divorce, the family members get very caught up in their own emotions, so that a little cat is left to emotionally fend for himself. He's already confused because he doesn't understand why a family member (either human or a pet) has suddenly disappeared. Next, he's aware of how different the remaining family members are behaving. He comes over to someone for comfort and is ignored. No one notices him at a time when he needs just as much comforting and reassurance as they do. In situations like a death in the family, normal routines are shattered, so the cat's meals may become irregular; grooming is neglected, so the coat gets matted. The cat eventually begins to feel invisible and knows there's no use in trying to seek out human companionship. He begins to keep to himself. The depression grows. I know that in such a serious crisis such as a death, it may seem trivial to be worrying about brushing your cat or keeping up with playtime. Believe me, it isn't trivial. It's essential because you can't explain to your cat what has happened to the family. All he knows is that someone he loved is gone and he's in mourning just as you are. Yes, cats do mourn. And, while you'll be receiving comfort from friends and family through visits, kind notes and phone calls, your cat has only one source of comfort...you. Even if it's difficult, try to keep his schedule as normal as possible. Now more than ever he needs that stress-relieving Play Therapy, good nutrition, regular grooming, and lots of comforting affection.

Depression caused by a major crisis is easy to diagnose. But it doesn't have to be such an obvious crisis to send your cat sliding into a depression. And, it's these more subtle situations that are harder to recognize. Let me give you an example. You've just been promoted at work and your schedule gets crazy. You barely have enough time for yourself, let alone find extra moments to play with your cat. You start coming home from work later and later. The pressure of this new job is taking its toll on your patience. When you walk in the door your cat starts meowing, following you around, walking in and out between your legs and getting in the way. You don't mean to but you yell at him. The meals you used to so lovingly prepare for him are now spooned out cold into his dish and placed on the floor. You pat him on the head and disappear into another room to go through your mail. After his meal, your cat comes in and jumps up on the papers you're trying to read. He just wants his usual dose of affection and play, but you push him off and promise you'll spend time with him in a little while.

You may periodically find time for your cat but it's very irregular and it's not the way he remembers. Repeatedly rejected, he becomes lonely and starts detaching himself from you by spending more and more time sleeping or looking out the window. He stops greeting you at the door. He doesn't come into the kitchen and eat when you call him for dinner. Eventually, when you find time to play those favorite games, he no longer responds.

Your cat may also go into a depression when left in a boarding kennel. Not only is he separated from his family but he's removed from his comforting environment and placed in a facility surrounded by strange cats and people. Some cats adjust to being boarded with no problems but there are some very sensitive cats who react more dramatically—unsure if the family is ever coming back.

Depression can start a chain reaction that can lead to poor appetite, lethargy, and a decline in hygiene. The immune system weakens, leaving the cat susceptible to illness. If you're caught up in other things you may not be aware of the initial signs when the depression crosses over into a medical condition.

Recognizing the Signs of Depression

Pay attention to your cat's normal behavior, personality and daily routine when all's right in his world. This way you stand a better chance of noticing when something changes.

Appetite
Be aware of his appetite under normal conditions. By monitoring his usual food intake you'll spot it right away when his appetite starts to fall off. A depressed cat has little desire for his dinner.

Activity/Play
What's your cat's normal playtime routine? Is he normally athletic and a ball of fire? Knowing his usual activity level and playtime habits will help you to notice if he's becoming more sedentary and not as enthusiastic toward his favorite games.

Sleep
Be familiar with your cat's sleeping patterns. In general, cats tend to sleep quite a bit during the day, but observe the specifics of your cat's sleep preferences. Should he begin to sleep more than usual, you'll be alerted. Depressed cats sleep more.

Grooming
How fastidious is your cat normally? A decrease in personal hygiene can be a sign of depression.

Personality
Do you know how sociable your cat is in general? Is he very affectionate or does he prefer to be close but not too close? Look for personality changes such as a normally sociable cat preferring to hide when

company comes, or an affectionate cat who no longer seeks out companionship.

Overall Appearance

Study your cat's face and body so you'll be able to notice even a subtle change. For instance, if you know how bright and alert his eyes normally appear you'll be able to notice if they've lost some of their sparkle. How solid does your cat's body feel? Would you be able to detect a loss of weight? How shiny is your cat's coat? How much does he normally shed?

Helping the Depressed Cat

- Have your cat examined by the vet to rule out any medical condition and also to determine if a secondary medical problem has developed due to the depression.
- If the depression is due to the death of a companion pet, be reassuring by providing lots of Play Therapy and affection. Remember, your cat is mourning the loss of his friend just as you are. In some cases, the addition of a new kitten can help but make sure you've worked on his self-confidence first (through Play Therapy and affection). If your cat depended on the companionship of his roommate then he'll probably appreciate a new friend. It's a decision you need to make based on your specific situation.
- For depression triggered by the loss of a family member or pet (either death, divorce, child moving out) it's essential that you try your best to not let your cat absorb your negative emotions. Cats are acutely aware of their owners' feelings. Go overboard with Play Therapy, praise, and attention. Make your cat feel like he's getting

more attention now than when the other family member was present.

- For the depression that crept up due to your change in lifestyle (job promotion, new relationship, etc.) you need to make time for your cat and never rebuff his attempts to be affectionate. Losing an extra fifteen minutes of sleep to play his favorite game is a small price to pay toward rebuilding the bond you and your cat once had. If your new job creates a completely erratic schedule, consider having a pet sitter come in regularly to not only feed your cat but provide playtime. For a single cat, this would be the perfect time to adopt a companion cat.

- In the case of divorce in a multicat household, try to keep the cats together if they're all best buddies. If the cats must be separated, keep their security in mind by letting them live with the person they're closest to.

- In all cases of depression use lots of touch, affection, Play Therapy and communication. Talk to your cat when you don't have the time to touch. When you're busily getting dressed for work, tell your cat how you'll look forward to seeing him that night, and mention his name often.

- Add some spice to a boring existence. Buy some new toys. If you've been neglecting those catnip parties, then indulge your cat. Leave some interesting objects around for your cat to investigate during your absence, such as a cardboard box with one of your shirts inside. Your scent on the clothing will be very comforting and what cat can resist cuddling up in a box? Leave an open paper bag around with a new toy inside for your cat to discover. If you feel like splurging you can buy him a cat tree. Put that sparkle back in your cat's eyes. Don't make light of feline depression or feel embarrassed to ask your vet about it. Some owners find it too silly to ask for help when they believe their cat is suffering from depression. Cats are very sensitive. If left untreated, depression can not only damage your relationship with him, it can escalate into a potentially serious medical condition.

chapter 11

Introducing a Companion Pet

One question I'm often asked is if all cats benefit from having a companion. The answer is no. Cats who are extremely people oriented and possessive of their owners probably won't benefit from the added competition. While the addition of a younger cat can spark a geriatric cat to enjoy life a bit more, some very old or ill cats may not benefit from having a newcomer around. In these cases it's best to check with your vet because he or she knows your individual cat's history. Some very ill cats don't need the added stress brought on by the introduction of a newcomer.

Introducing a Second Cat

Cats are territorial animals so you need to prepare yourself for some complaints from your resident cat when a second one is brought onto her turf. With the proper preparation beforehand and the right introduction, you'll be able to soften the blow and make it an easier transition for both cats. Despite their territoriality, cats can benefit from the companionship, and bringing a second cat home can be just the spark that a bored and lonely cat needs.

If you're thinking about getting a buddy for your cat, it helps if you can find one with a complementary personality. I know that isn't always an easy thing to do but if possible, it could mean a faster acceptance of each other. The following list gives some examples.

Complementary Personalities

Your Cat	New Cat	Benefits
lap cat	playful, not a lap cat	There won't be so much competition for your attention. Less jealousy.
obese cat	kitten (about 3 months old)	This will get your cat to enjoy life more. Playtime will come back to her.
hyperactive cat	a young cat (about 6 month old)	Good for playtime.
lonely cat	any cat who prefers other cats over people; not a lap cat.	Offers companionship and closeness.

Your adult cat should be neutered or spayed before introducing another cat. Neutering reduces feelings of territoriality. In general, kittens pose the least threat to an adult cat's sense of territory. If your cat is an adult you might do best by adopting a kitten of the opposite sex.

Before the Introduction
Bring home some paper that has the new cat's scent on it and leave strips around the house. Don't go making a big deal out of it, just casually drop the strips in different spots. This helps your cat begin to get used to the scent of the new cat.

When your cat seems pretty cool about the paper strips then bring home a piece of cloth material that's been rubbed over the new cat.

Place this cloth somewhere in the house. This will have a stronger scent than the paper strips and will allow your cat to do a more thorough investigation. You can also rub your cat down with a cloth and bring it to the new cat to help him get acquainted.

Not everyone will have the luxury of this much time needed to do the paper strips and cloth routine. If your new cat can't remain in his current home long enough for you to do this, then don't worry about it, just move on to the next step.

Before ever introducing a new cat into your household, the cat should be brought to the vet for feline leukemia testing. Testing for parasites (such as ear mites, worms, etc.) should also be done because you don't want to bring anything home that can be spread to your own cat. If the cat hasn't been vaccinated, now would be the time to begin that. Also, make sure your resident cat is up-to-date on her vaccinations before bringing home a new kitty.

Have both cats' nails trimmed before the introduction to lessen any damage that might be done by a paw swipe.

Feed both cats beforehand as this will help toward a calmer reaction.

The Introduction
If possible, have someone other than yourself bring the new cat into the house. Because cats are territorial, if you aren't the one bringing the "intruder" in, your cat won't feel quite so betrayed. Perhaps you can get a neighbor to help out. All your neighbor will have to do is bring the cat into the house and set him up in a room you've designated as the newcomer's temporary territory. This room should be set up with a litter box, bed, food bowl, water and toys just for the newcomer. The door should of course remain closed.

While the neighbor is setting up the new cat in his room, you should be distracting your cat with playtime. Don't try to hold and comfort her because if she's very upset you'll end up getting scratched or bitten. Just use your Cat Dancer or Kitty Tease to distract her. Don't be too offended if she ignores you.

When the neighbor is finished, she should casually leave. You act as if nothing unusual is going on. Your cat may go over to the newcomer's door and sniff.

She may even growl and hiss. Don't get excited; this is normal behavior. Continue to act as if you had nothing to do with this and you have no idea how a cat got into your house.

Keep the newcomer in the separate room for a few days until things quiet down. This helps him to adjust to his new surroundings and gives your resident cat some time to get over the initial shock of having an intruder in her territory. It's an easier transition for your cat this way because only a portion of her turf has been violated.

You'll naturally have to go into the new cat's room to feed him, change the litter, etc., but it's very important that you limit your contact with him initially. The more your cat smells the newcomer on your hands or clothing, the more upset she'll be with you. After handling the newcomer, wash your hands before touching your cat. I often tell clients to keep an old robe in the newcomer's room so you can hold him without getting his scent on your clothes. Then just take the robe off before going back out to your cat. Note: If your resident cat is just a kitten and you're introducing an older cat into the household, you can go ahead and give lots of attention to the new cat. Your kitten will not have developed her territorial tendencies yet and the new cat will be needing more support.

Give your cat lots of extra attention during this time. The tone of your voice is a valuable tool here also. Talk soothingly to your cat about the benefits of having a companion. Don't underestimate the power of talking to your cat. She can pick up on your emotions quite easily. If you're nervous and have an edge to your voice, she'll know there's cause for alarm. On the other hand, if your tone is calm and reassuring, she'll be more inclined to relax.

If things seem relatively calm, change the cats' positions for a few hours. Let your cat go into the newcomer's room to check things out for herself. At the same time, let the newcomer out to explore another room in the house. Having an assistant during this stage is very helpful because you should stay with your cat. Afterward, return the cats to their original areas.

If things seem calm, the next day casually open the new cat's door and allow the two to make initial contact. Remember, the key is to *casually* open the door. Supervise from a distance. Don't interfere unless a battle is about to take place. Hissing, growling, and even a paw swipe are to be expected. Screaming isn't a good sign. Separate the cats if full-fledged screaming is going on.

Even though the newcomer will now have full access to the house, leave his litter box and bed set up in his room. He may need the security of that original home base for a while. It may also help speed acceptance if he's using his own litter box for a bit longer and leaving your cat's box alone. Later, if all goes well you may be able to eliminate the second box if the newcomer starts using your resident cat's box without causing any commotion. Be prepared, though. Some cats object to sharing their litter boxes and if your cat is one of those, you may always have to keep two boxes available.

Acceptance can take anywhere from a few days to a month or

more. You can greatly increase the chance of success by not petting the new kitty for a while. This forces him to seek out your cat for companionship. Mention your cat's name often and talk to her in soothing tones every time you do something for the new kitty. Talking to your resident cat lets her feel included. You'll know it's okay to pet the newcomer when your resident cat begins to let him come relatively close without swiping or running away. The very best signs of success are playing or sleeping together and grooming each other. I remember how happy I felt when I saw my resident cat, Albert, sitting right next to a recent addition to my family, Olive. They were just looking out the window sharing a much cherished (by Albert) sunny spot in the living room. They soon settled down for a nap, curling up very close together. I knew things were going to be okay from then on and that Olive had passed the test.

Whenever the two cats are together, make their time positive. Use the Cat Dancer or Kitty Tease to encourage playtime. The Cat Dancer can also be used to defuse trouble. Keep it curled up and stashed conveniently nearby so you can get it easily if you see one cat start to go for the other. Distracting the aggressor from the potential attack will allow her to work out her energy on the toy and leave your other cat safe and calm.

Mealtime can be used to your advantage when it comes to bringing cats together. At first you may have to feed them separately to avoid growling and hissing. Gradually, move the bowls closer each day. (Don't rush it; you may only be able to move them an inch closer each time.) Once you get them eating in the same room you can give yourself a great big pat on the back because that's a huge step toward acceptance. When the cats are eating in the same room, move the bowls very slowly toward each other—I mean half an inch a day if necessary. Never move them close enough to have the two cats within swatting range. You want each cat to feel secure and not threatened. Eventually you may be able to move the bowls side by side but that will depend on your individual cats. You may have to settle for them just being able to eat in the same room. A small victory is still a victory!

Adopting a Third Cat

Bringing a third cat into a household can create a situation where two bond and become friends, leaving one cat feeling rejected. If you do decide to adopt a third cat, make certain you have enough room so that each cat can have territorial security. To help avoid territorial disputes, you can expand the size of the cats' environment just by creating multilevel areas through the use of perches, cat trees, boxes, etc. This will help give each cat more personal territory.

You'll also have to be watchful and remain sensitive toward the changing dynamics of the relationships. Make sure one cat isn't being left out or picked on. If so, she'll need lots of extra attention from you and you'll need to use playtime with the Kitty Tease or Cat Dancer to encourage all the cats to bond.

At least two litter boxes will always be needed, even after the initial introduction. Ideally, one box for each cat is best but not everyone has room for three litter boxes. Three cats sharing one box will get smelly too fast and you could then end up with an indiscriminate urination problem as the cats seek cleaner accommodations. Having two or three boxes will also help avoid one cat having to cross another's territory to use the litter.

Mealtime becomes trickier when there are three or more cats. Making sure each kitty gets her share of food and that mealtime goes smoothly isn't always easy. Watch that nobody gets nosed out of the food bowl. If necessary, feed each cat far enough away from others to ease anxiety.

Introducing a New Cat into a Dog's Household

Introducing a cat into a dog's territory is easier than you'd expect because dogs are pack animals.

If you have a large dog, the cat you adopt should be at least three or four months old. If your dog is shy and quiet, adopt a less energetic cat. Old dogs will also appreciate a less energetic cat. A shy or elderly dog doesn't need a motorized "in your face" kind of cat scaring him during his much needed nap time. An energetic, hyper dog shouldn't be paired up with a shy and timid cat. Try to complement the personalities and don't be too impulsive.

If you choose to adopt an adult cat, if possible, make sure she hasn't had any bad experiences with dogs in the past. Also, some adult cats who're never been around a dog may be very fearful. Adopting a kitten that is three or four months old will usually work out best because she won't have the fear of dogs that an adult cat may have.

Before the Introduction
If possible, bring home a cloth material (such as a T-shirt) with the new cat's scent on it to help familiarize your dog with his soon-to-be companion. You can also bring a scented cloth to the new cat.

Have a room set up for the new cat with her litter box, food bowl, water, bed, and toys. Even after the cat and dog are comfortable with each other you'll want to make sure the dog can't get to the litter box (some dogs take great pleasure in seeking out and ingesting cat feces).

Trim everyone's nails before introduction time and feed a good dinner. Both animals will be calmer if they have full stomachs.

The Introduction

There's no need to have someone else bring the cat in (the method needed to introduce two cats to each other). Your dog will respond best with you bringing the newcomer in because he'll look for your guidance. Have the cat in a carrier that will allow both animals to see each other. If your dog is uncontrollable or a bit too excitable, keep him on a leash. You might even need to speak to your veterinarian about using a mild tranquilizer during the introduction phase. An assistant would be a big help during this time. Call in a favor and ask a friend or neighbor to lend a hand.

No matter how well or how badly things go, it's important that you stay calm. If you get upset or excited you'll rev up your dog even more and that in turn will make the cat nervous.

After a few minutes you should set up the new cat in her own room and close the door. Then, go out and play with your dog.

Provided the newcomer is secure enough, after a few days you can have the cat and dog switch rooms for an hour or so. This helps the dog to get used to the cat's scent and gives the cat a chance to explore her new home. She'll also be spreading her scent throughout the house, which is important. If possible, have an assistant during this process. You can stay in the room with your dog and the assistant can supervise the cat.

The first few times you allow the cat and dog to meet, have the dog on a leash so you can control any potential problems. Praise your dog every time he responds positively to the cat. If your dog is normally a bit too excitable, you should take him out to play before having him meet the cat. This way he'll be a little tired out and will respond more calmly. Remember, praise the dog and tell him how good he is when he's tolerant and accepting of the cat. Your dog is highly motivated to please you.

When things go consistently well and you're comfortable with how the dog and cat react to each other, leave the door to the cat's room open. Put up a gate to keep the dog out so the cat can go in for safety or privacy if desired. Keep a squirt bottle (filled with plain water) handy in case an unexpected fight breaks out. You don't want to reach in and try to separate the two because you could easily get injured.

When you aren't going to be around to supervise, you need to put the cat back into her room with the door closed. Don't leave the dog alone with the cat until you're *absolutely* sure they've accepted each other and there's no chance of a tragedy.

To help your dog accept his new companion, give him lots of extra attention to avoid jealousy. Help him realize that his new friend is a plus for him and not a minus. The newcomer will need attention too, so help her adjust to these sometimes overwhelming surroundings.

Always allow the cat to have a place to jump up to for safety, away from the dog. If you're not going to permit her on the furniture be certain she has her own cat tree that's out of the dog's reach.

Introducing a Dog into Your Cat's Household

Before the Introduction

Accustom your cat to the sound of a dog beforehand by playing a tape of barking sounds a few times daily (for short intervals) for at least a few weeks. You can usually get a dog-owning friend or neighbor to make a tape for you. Start with the volume on low and gradually work up so you don't startle your poor kitty.

You may want to raise your cat's feeding area off the floor so she won't be disturbed during mealtime. Doing this before the dog arrives helps your cat get used to the location change under peaceful conditions.

Make sure the litter box is off limits to the dog by either buying a covered box, elevating it a bit, or installing a gate that your cat can jump over but the dog can't.

Keep a gate on hand in case you need to confine the dog. This may help to allow your cat an occasional breather from an anxious pup.

Trim nails before the introduction and serve dinner to encourage a calm reaction.

The Introduction

Have the dog on a leash so you can control him. You can follow many of the instructions given in the previous section on "Introducing a New Cat Into a Dog's Household," just modify them as needed. For instance, instead of keeping the cat in a separate room, you'll be confining the dog. If you're adopting a young puppy, talk to your veterinarian on how to house train the newcomer.

Even though a new dog in the house is a lot of fun (especially a puppy) and demands much of your time, don't neglect your cat. She'll need lots of extra attention now so she won't feel left out. Find time for all the usual games and don't neglect her regular grooming schedule.

Don't leave the cat and dog unsupervised until you're positive they've accepted each other completely.

chapter 12

Cats and Their Human Families

So many times an owner will call me in a panic because she is expecting a baby and someone has told her that she has to get rid of the cat. You can always count on at least one "friend" telling the tale of how cats steal the breath from babies or how they cause miscarriages. Owners also call me because they're convinced they must declaw their cats in case they become insanely jealous and intentionally harm the baby.

Cats smothering babies is an old wives' tale and one which I wish would stop resurfacing. There's no truth to it and that's that!

As for the miscarriages, there is a danger of pregnant women contracting toxoplasmosis and passing it along to the fetus. You are at more risk of becoming infected with toxoplasmosis by handling raw meat than you'd ever be from your cat. There are some precautions, though, that you need to be aware of. I'll go over them in this chapter so you'll be able to protect yourself and your unborn baby.

Jealousy can be a concern when it comes to bringing home a new baby or any other person (or pet) who'll be receiving your attention. With some awareness and preplanning on your part to help your cat adjust, jealousy may never even be an issue. As for cats intentionally harming babies—no way. But we'll look into that more closely a little further on.

Toxoplasmosis

This disease is caused by the protozoan parasite toxoplasma gondii. The cat becomes infected by eating prey that's contaminated by the parasite. Microscopic eggs (called oocysts) are shed in the infected cat's feces. This is why you've probably heard that pregnant women shouldn't clean the litter box. Toxoplasmosis can cause severe damage to the fetus. There's no cause for panic, though, because once the eggs are shed in the feces it takes a couple of days for them to reach the infectious stage. So prompt scooping out of the fecal waste will greatly reduce the chance of infection. To be on the safe side, pregnant women should have another family member handle litter box duties. At the very least, wear gloves (you can buy a box of disposable latex gloves from a medical supply company) and wash your hands afterward.

Indoor cats are at very low risk for toxoplasmosis. Outdoor cats are more likely to acquire the disease due to the hunting and ingesting of potentially infected prey. Indoor cats are at risk if you allow them to eat raw or undercooked meat.

Humans are more likely to become infected by handling raw meat and then handling vegetables that are to be eaten raw. However, most adult humans have built up an immunity to toxoplasmosis. If you're at all worried (especially if you're pregnant), take your cat to the veterinarian to be tested for toxoplasmosis. In the meantime, here are some precautions for reducing your chance of developing toxoplasmosis:

- Never allow your cat to eat raw meat.
- Keep your cat indoors so he won't be able to catch and eat prey.
- Wash your hands after handling raw meat and thoroughly clean all work surfaces. Don't prepare raw vegetables on the same surface you use to prepare meat. Also, thoroughly wash all utensils used to prepare raw meat before preparing vegetables.
- Remove fecal waste from the litter box right away. Don't allow it to sit in the box for days. Wash your hands after cleaning the litter box. Pregnant women should assign another family member the litter box duty. If that's not possible, wear gloves.
- Teach young children not to play around the litter box.
- Wear gloves when doing outdoor gardening.
- Don't allow children to play in public park sandboxes (stray cats

may have used it as a litter box). If you have a sandbox in your yard keep it covered.

- If you allow your cat on the kitchen counter, clean the surface before beginning any food preparation (not so much because of the danger of toxoplasmosis, but so your guests won't end up eating Fettucini à la Cat Hair).

Before the Baby Arrives

Your cat is used to being the only baby in the house. In a few months his world is going to drastically change. Cats don't care too much for change. They take great comfort in familiarity. To avoid the potential problem of jealousy (actually, it won't be jealousy as much as it will be anxiety), you should start now to help your cat adjust to the changes that'll be taking place and preparing him in a positive way for the new arrival.

- If your cat hasn't been spayed or neutered, have that done before the baby arrives. Intact cats have a lower anxiety threshold and bringing a new baby home will certainly cause anxiety. Intact males in particular have a strong territorial sense and the anxiety caused by the new arrival could trigger episodes of urine spraying.
- Use baby powder and baby oil on yourself so your cat starts getting used to how the baby's going to smell. This way the powder scent on the baby will be familiar to him.
- Make a tape of a baby crying and other baby sounds (surely you know someone with a baby who'll cooperate). Play the tape regularly. Start it at a very low volume and over the course of a few weeks gradually increase it (never play it loud, though). Whenever you play the tape you should comfort your cat, stroking him and talking in reassuring tones. Don't force your cat to stay if he chooses to run when the tape's on. Just keep the volume very low and go about your daily routine as usual. Play Therapy sessions are also important now (refer to Chapter 4).
- As you begin to purchase baby furniture let your cat investigate. If you're assembling pieces, take frequent breaks to play with your cat so he doesn't feel left out.
- If you start adding furniture, do it slowly, and allow your cat to be part of the nursery. Then he won't feel threatened and overwhelmed. Bringing in each addition gradually allows him time to adjust to an unfamiliar piece.
- Don't paint the nursery, carpet it, and add the new furniture all in a week or two. The room will be totally foreign to him and he could become threatened. As you do each step, give him time to become familiar.

- If your cat tries to sleep in the empty crib you can use empty soda cans with a few pennies inside (tape over the opening). Set up the cans inside the crib and line them along the railings. Your cat won't like the sound they make. Keep the cans set up until the baby arrives. By using the cans instead of you yelling at the cat, he won't feel you're the one denying him access to a place that he feels should be his. He'll come to the conclusion on his own that the crib isn't all that great a spot to sleep in.
- If you have a friend or neighbor with a baby, invite them over for a visit to help your cat adjust to the sight, sound, and smell. Talk to your cat in soothing tones during the visit and don't force him to interact with the baby.
- As the baby's arrival time gets nearer, be sure you're not neglecting all the rituals you and your cat share. Don't forget his grooming, playtime, stroking and petting sessions, catnip parties, etc.
- Don't run out and declaw your cat. So many people feel they have to do this in order to prevent a baby from being scratched. A cat will only scratch if he feels he's in danger. Declawing him can make him more insecure because you've taken away his warning system. Declawing a cat is traumatic. When you add in the arrival of a new baby it can cause a stress overload. He could become more inclined to bite as a result. Cats with claws do very well around babies and children. Keeping your cat's nails trimmed will help.

When the Baby Comes Home
- Feed your cat his favorite meal so he'll feel satisfied.
- Lavish attention on your cat. Everyone will want to "ooh and ahh" over the baby but your cat needs to feel loved and special too.
- Let the cat sniff the baby's things.
- If your cat is calm you can let him sniff the baby. It's important that you remain calm or else your cat will pick up on your anxiety. Don't force the baby on your cat. Let him set the pace.
- If your cat chooses to run and hide don't chase after him. He'll eventually peek his nose back into the room and when he does, welcome him with a reassuring, calm tone of voice.
- Talk to your cat and mention his name as you do things for the baby. Then he'll feel a part of the process. This will be especially helpful if you can't physically comfort him —the verbal communication is the next best thing.
- Even though you may not feel much like playing, a Play Therapy session will be a great stress reliever for your cat (and probably for you, too). It will help him realize that things haven't changed all that much.

- Some extra support from vitamins B and C may be very helpful at this time. Refer to Chapter 9. Your cat will naturally be curious about the strange-looking arrival. Let him interact with the baby under your close (but casual-appearing) supervision. While the baby is nursing the cat may pick up on the feelings of contentment and choose to sleep nearby.

To allow you more freedom to spend enough private time with your cat you can purchase a nursery monitor. This will allow you to keep an ear tuned to the baby while being in another room to perhaps do some grooming or a Play Therapy session.

If you're concerned about your cat's reaction to the baby or if he loves the baby so much he wants to visit the crib all the time you can get a special net that fits over the top of the crib. These nets are available at baby supply stores. If you prefer to keep the cat out of the nursery completely, consider replacing the regular door with a screen door so he can look in at the baby and continue to become acquainted with the scents and sounds. It really makes a difference if you don't totally shut him out of this new family experience.

If your kitty believes he's getting his regular amount of attention (though you actually should be giving him more attention just to be on the safe side), he'll be less inclined to view the new baby as a threat. If he feels his position in the family is secure, you won't encounter such things as territorial urine marking. If your cat does start spraying (mostly males will do this but your female cat may resort to urine marking), don't use punishment. Punishment will create more anxiety in your cat. For ill-placed litter box attempts, don't use any form of punishment. A little attention, affection and patience is what he needs as he makes the adjustment. Use the techniques described in Chapter 6 for serious litter box problems. The spraying of urine on baby things can also be a marking behavior done out of affection to claim the baby as a part of the cat's family.

For a cat who becomes very anxious over the arrival of a new baby, keep an eye on the litter box. Make sure your cat is urinating in the box. Some cats can get so stressed out that they develop a case of cystitis (especially if they've had it before). Watch for signs of frequent trips to the litter box, crying or straining while urinating, voiding little or no urine each time, frequent licking of genital area, blood in urine, urinating small amounts outside of the box, or depression. Consult your veterinarian immediately.

As the Children Grow

If you're consistent in teaching your children how to treat your cat with love and respect, they'll learn to view him as a member of the family and not a moving toy. In return, your cat won't view your children as enemies to be avoided at all cost.

When the relationship blossoms, both cat and child benefit. Cats can be of great comfort to a lonely or ill child. They're endlessly patient listeners and gentle companions. Children can be great playmates and loving friends for cats.

- Teach the proper handling of animals. If your child grabs a tail or a fistful of fur, gently get him to let go and pet your cat to demonstrate how softly an animal is to be petted. Your petting the cat will also calm and reassure him.
- Teach a child to pet with an open hand. Also, instruct that petting should be done with one hand only so the cat never feels restrained.
- Loud toys such as pistols, jack-in-the-boxes, talking toys, remote control cars, etc., can be absolutely terrifying to a little cat. Teach your child to play with these toys far away from the cat and to never surprise a sleeping kitty with such sudden noises.
- Keep the litter box out of a child's reach. You certainly don't want curious little fingers playing in the litter. A covered box might be a good idea at this time. It also allows your cat some privacy.
- As children begin to crawl you want to make sure they can't get into the cat's food or water bowl. Besides the mess it causes, your cat needs to feel his feeding area is secure and quiet. Don't allow a child to disturb kitty during mealtime.
- When children are old enough they can help with caring for the cat, but don't leave the responsibility for an animal's welfare to a child. You need to keep track of the litter box habits, monitor food intake, do periodic home health exams, be aware of mood fluctuations, and all the other aspects of pet care that are too subtle for a child to notice.
- I've found that providing books about cats for children helps them in learning about respect and understanding for all animals in addition to their own pet. There are several books written especially for children. I also recommend subscribing to one of the monthly magazines such as *Cat Fancy*. Children love looking at the pictures and reading the stories people write about their own cats. You can encourage your child to write to the magazine with any questions about cat care. It's always exciting for a child to see his letter published and he'll be learning something in the process.

Cat Fancy has a section in each magazine just for children. Magazine addresses are listed in the Appendix.

Introducing a New Person into Your Cat's Household

As in the previous section on preparing a cat for a new baby's arrival, the key is to make certain your cat feels that none of the attention he's used to getting will be sacrificed for the sake of the newcomer.

Before the Person Moves In
- If it hasn't already been done, have your cat spayed or neutered. Unstable hormones can play havoc with a cat's anxiety level.
- Have the person visit at dinner time so he or she can feed the cat.
- We're not above bribery here so have the person bring a new toy every so often (perhaps an irresistible peacock feather).
- Throw a catnip party during these visits.
- Don't push the new person on the cat. Let your kitty go at his own pace. If he prefers not to be held or petted, just let him control how close he wants to get. You'll make much more progress if your cat doesn't feel threatened or cornered.
- Have the person leave a few scented articles of clothing around to help your cat get acquainted with his or her scent. This is an important step. Don't have the person move in without going through this stage for at least a few weeks. This truly can mean the difference between a smooth transition or a traumatic nightmare when it comes time for the person's belongings to be moved in.
- The person should participate in Play Therapy sessions with your cat. If necessary, you may have to start the game. Then, as your cat becomes more comfortable have the other person take over. Maybe you can discover a toy that can be a special game exclusively between your cat and the other person.
- The person should spend time sitting on the floor so he or she is on the cat's level. Remember that most of the time the only things a cat gets to see are shoes and ankles. Let the cat come up and investigate. The person should remain casual and let the cat initiate all interaction. You and the person should continue to engage in casual conversation so the cat doesn't feel he's being watched.

When the Person Moves In
- Try to make the move as peaceful as possible. Put your cat in a safe area of the house if the move involves lots of boxes coming in. You don't want him to get accidentally injured or let out the door.

- During unpacking, take several breaks to play with your cat (especially if the person has devised a special game for the cat).
- The person should continue the practice of getting down on the floor to be on the cat's level.
- Some extra support from vitamins B and C may be helpful at this time. Specifics can be found in Chapter 9.

Jealousy of Your New Spouse

Oh, this can be a sensitive issue. It just takes support and patience, so don't give up. Cats tend to have more problems with new husbands than new wives. One reason may be the deeper, louder sound of the male's voice. Another can be the type of cologne the man uses. Musk type colognes have chemical ingredients that resemble male pheromones which can represent a challenge to a male cat.

To help your cat overcome jealous feelings toward your new spouse, here are some tips:
- Have your spouse take over feeding duties but make sure he or she does it the way your cat is used to.
- Start Play Therapy games and then let your spouse take over.
- Lavish attention on your cat and make sure his time with you hasn't been reduced.
- Throw weekly catnip parties when your spouse is there.
- For new husbands: Don't wear the musk type cologne. Also, try to keep a quiet, calm tone of voice around the cat. This is especially important if the cat hasn't had much exposure to men.
- Purchase an ionizer to help send out those wonderful negative ions. Refer to Chapter 9 for specifics on the benefits of ionizers.
- Mention your cat's name often to help him feel a part of things.
- Try to be aware of your type of movements throughout the house. A cat raised in a household of men may find the sounds and movements a woman makes very alarming. The same is true for new husbands. The broader movements or heavier footsteps can be scary for the kitty.
- If your cat has favorite places in the house be sure your spouse knows this and won't intrude on them. For instance: If your cat sleeps in the chair by the fireplace every night after dinner then it certainly won't help family/cat relations if your spouse suddenly starts sitting there after dinner. Your spouse should get another chair and put it close to the cat's chair. This way the cat may choose to sit in his own spot or sit in your spouse's lap.
- Continue having your spouse spend time at the cat's level by sitting on the floor.

• Vitamins B and C may be supplemented in the diet as needed. Above all else, be patient and positive toward your cat. This is a big adjustment for everyone in the family and your cat needs to be eased into the change.

chapter 13

Bringing the Great Outdoors Inside

Let's face it, while you'd love your cat to experience sunshine, grass, fresh air, and all the other joys of outdoor life, the reality is that it also includes cars, dogs, poisons, severe weather, other cats, cruel people, theft, fleas, ticks, and infectious diseases. For many cats, the advantages may not outweigh the disadvantages. Sometimes, a once safe environment changes because a strange dog starts roaming around or a tough new tomcat moves into the neighborhood. Often what causes an owner to restrict his or her cat to the indoors is a move to a new house. Perhaps the new house is on a busy street with lots of traffic. Or maybe the move is to a city apartment. So there are times when an indoor/outdoor cat must make the transition to life exclusively indoors. That's when frustrated owners call me because they can no longer tolerate the sound of their cat constantly crying at the door. Some cats even climb up the window screens, trying to find a way out. You can't blame them. They don't understand why access to the outdoors has suddenly been denied.

Cats love the outdoors because it provides a constant source of stimulation. There are birds to watch and hopefully catch, mice to track down, lots of scents to investigate, and, for the more territorial cat, a yard that needs to be patrolled. Then there's that afternoon nap on the patio in the warm sun to recharge a hard-working kitty. Sounds good, doesn't it? Only your cat doesn't understand that an oncoming car may not stop in time for her to finish stalking that bird on the other side of the street. Your cat also doesn't understand that the tomcat she's about to encounter is maybe infected with the FTLV virus (for which there's no protective vaccine).

Based on your specific environment you may find you have to confine your indoor/outdoor cat to the inside only. To do that successfully means bringing the best of the outdoors inside—or as close as you can since I'm sure you don't want to drop a mouse or two on the living room carpet for your cat's enjoyment. As with any behavior modification, don't expect success right away. It'll take patience but the end result is well worth it. Brace yourself, though, because a cat used to outdoor life is going to cry at the door or window. Your job will be to create an "outdoor" environment inside while keeping your kitty safe and healthy.

To make life easier for you and most especially for your cat, the first thing that needs to be done if it hasn't been already, is to spay (or neuter). In addition to being healthier by reducing the risk of developing certain cancers later in life, it'll also make her adjustment to indoor life a smoother one, without all those surging hormones causing havoc with her emotions.

Owners commonly make the mistake when confining a cat indoors of providing no stimulation. Indoor cats tend to sleep a lot out of boredom. Boredom can lead to lethargy, obesity, excessive grooming (sometimes to the point of self-mutilation), frustration, poor or excessive appetite. In multicat households it can lead to increased aggression as cats begin to take out their frustrations on each other.

To create the illusion of the outdoors you have to provide a good tree or two. By a tree, I'm referring to an elevated place for a cat to climb and perch. It can be a homemade tree, or you can buy one at the pet supply store. Cat House Originals can create one for you according to your specifications and budget. Their address is in the Appendix. You can also have the "tree" be the top of a desk, the top of the refrigerator, or anywhere else you'll allow your cat to perch. Cats feel more secure off the ground so if you don't want to invest in a cat tree, at least allow her a few favorite perches. Then she can climb up and oversee her domain.

The Litter Box

Not all indoor/outdoor cats use litter boxes. Many owners have found it convenient to train their cats to go outdoors. If your cat has never used a litter box before and she objects to clay litter, you may have to use the sand litter (such as Ever Clean). In some cases you may even have to start off by using plain soil in the litter box. Then, after your cat has successfully made the transition you can gradually introduce clay or sand litter by mixing a little in with the soil. Over the course of a week or so you can increase the amount of litter while decreasing the amount of soil. Don't use scented litter. If your cat is used to digging in plain old dirt, her nose isn't going to enjoy being assaulted by all that perfume.

The litter box you choose should be large and uncovered. Things need to be as easy for her as possible during the adjustment period (once she has accepted the box and uses it without a problem you can put the cover on if you prefer). You may even need more than one box if you have a large house or more than one cat. For specifics on litter box problems, refer to Chapter 6.

The Scratching Post

Since your cat will no longer have access to her favorite tree trunks or fence posts to keep her claws in good shape and unkink tight muscles,

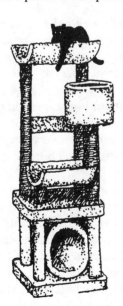

you'll have to provide a suitable replacement. The right kind of post is key to keeping your furniture from damage. Refer to Chapter 7 for specifics on the kind of post you'll need and how to train your cat to use it.

A Room with a View

Next we come to windows. An indoor cat loves to look out the window to watch birds go by and to keep an eye on the back yard. While you're helping a cat adjust to indoor life, access to certain windows may have to be restricted. If your cat was a tough defender of her territory, she may get too upset looking out the front window, watching intruding cats crossing her yard. If that's the case, keep the curtains closed or if necessary, put a temporary barrier up so the cat can't see out the window. Use distraction as a way to take her mind off what's happening outside and relieve her stress. Interactive toys and Play Therapy should be used for distraction.

If your cat doesn't have any problems with watching what goes on outside her window then by all means let her enjoy the view. It can be wonderful therapy for a bored cat. In fact, to make your cat even more comfortable you can buy a window shelf made especially for cats. If your local pet supply store doesn't carry them, they can be ordered from Hobar Manufacturing. See the Appendix for their address.

Boredom

If your cat just sleeps all the time now that she's confined indoors you'll need to provide stimulation. Refer to Chapter 4 on Play Therapy for instructions on providing scheduled playtime to ease boredom, frustration, or aggression. Play Therapy will also improve the bond between you and. your kitty. Play Therapy with interactive toys will satisfy the predator in your cat as you simulate the hunting and capturing of prey that she probably enjoyed outdoors. Leave some fun little toys around for your cat to enjoy on her own (such as a furry mouse or two, a ping-pong ball, an open paper bag). Rotate toys to prevent boredom.

Catnip will play an important role in easing boredom and helping your cat enjoy indoor life. Catnip and its role in behavior modification are covered in Chapter 4.

Some owners combat kitty boredom by installing a small aquarium for a cat's entertainment. I know many cats who enjoy aquariums. A note of caution, though: If you decide to set one up for your cat, make certain it's covered securely and there's no chance of your cat pushing it open. If you don't want to go to the trouble of getting an aquarium, check out one of the kitty videos available at pet supply stores. Some cats love them.

To avoid excessive eating or a decrease in appetite due to boredom, put your cat on scheduled mealtimes. Doing Play Therapy before meals helps stimulate a poor appetite.

If your cat is an only child and seems bored and lonely indoors, consider adopting a companion for her. A feline friend can be just what she needs if you're gone all day and she's stuck in the house. Chapter 11 covers how to do the proper introduction of a second cat.

Set up fun areas or cozy napping places for your kitty. In her previous outdoor life she probably had lots of spots to catch a snooze (such as under a bush or in a basket in the garage). Perhaps get one of those cute A-frame style beds (check Appendix) or line a basket with a towel or small pillow and set it in a sunny corner for her.

More Tips

- Protect your house plants by growing a pot of wheat grass for her to nibble on. See Chapter 5 for instructions.
- For a cat used to spending most of her time outdoors, begin by confining her inside for short periods at first. Gradually increase the time spent indoors.
- Use an ionizer/air purifier to keep the air clean. This will help any family members who are allergic to cats. The ionizer is also important for supplying an abundance of negative ions in the air. Negative ions help your moods. More on ionizers in chapter 9.
- Keep a few Cat Dancers stashed away in different parts of the house so there'll always be one handy in case you have to distract your cat away from something.
- Give your cat some time to learn her indoor manners. Use positive reinforcement and the behavior modification techniques described in this book to teach her what's acceptable and what isn't.
- Even though your cat is now an indoor cat, continue to keep her up-to-date on vaccinations.
- If you're going to leave windows open for your cat to enjoy, be sure all the screens are secure. A persistent cat will make short work of a flimsy screen or one that isn't fastened securely.

chapter 14

Reaching Out
Adopting an Abused or Abandoned Cat

cat doesn't have to display physical signs of abuse or neglect (such as bruises, wounds, broken bones) for him to have suffered traumatically. Emotional trauma covers a wide range of experience. It can be the reaction to a normal and often necessary change such as a move to a new house, new baby, new spouse, etc. These changes can be traumatic for most cats, but often, with support and extra love on your part, a cat normally adjusts in a relatively short amount of time. The kind of trauma I want to talk about is the severe result of abuse, neglect, abandonment, being hit by a car, a dog attack, being lost, or having lived in a violent environment. These are the special cats who, when we adopt or rescue them, require a tremendous amount of patience and a gentle kind of love to enable them to begin to trust again.

Rescuing a cat who so desperately needs a second chance can be one of the most unselfish things you can do because you know from the very start that there'll be so much emotional damage in need of repair. And, in the case of physical injuries, you know there'll be a long road ahead in terms of recovery. Taking on something like this involves serious thought as to the time and emotional commitment involved. Most people want a happy, well-adjusted cat who'll recognize how much he's loved by his owner. A cat who has previously been abused, abandoned, or who had to fend for himself for so long may always retain some emotional scars even after all the physical wounds have healed.

Once you get the cat he should be examined by the vet before you bring him into your home for rehabilitation. Even if the cat shows no physical signs of injury he'll need to be examined and tested for FELV and FTLV. In most cases this is easier said than done, but let me assure you that the sooner you're able to get the cat to the vet, the better. Even if you have to capture the cat in a humane trap to bring him in, he'll need an initial examination. (You can also use a dog crate with fishing line tied to the door. Place food in the crate. When the cat goes in, you can shut the door from a distance by pulling the line. Depending on his condition and age, he may be able to be tranquilized to be examined or treated (if injured). I know it sounds like you'll be putting the poor cat through even more trauma by taking him to the vet, but you need to know what you're dealing with for this to be a successful rehabilitation. He may even be able to be neutered at that time. He stands a better chance of success if he's not at the mercy of his hormones, so if he can be neutered that'll help the effort tremendously. You also need to know if he has an infectious disease in case you have other cats at home to consider. Talk to your vet; he or she will advise you on how much should be done based on the individual cat's specific case.

Gaining Trust

When you bring the cat into the house, put him in an unused room where he can remain for the next several weeks (or even months) during his physical and/or emotional rehabilitation. Have a litter box set up for him there. Don't use a covered box because he may only be used to outdoor gardens and dirt. Use plain litter so there'll be no perfume scent to confuse him. In the case of a cat with physical injuries (such as a splinted leg), be sure to use a litter box with very low sides for easy access. Be tolerant of failed litter box attempts.

I'm sure the first thing the cat will do when you place him in the room will be to run for cover. Let him hide under the bed or in the closet if he prefers. If the room doesn't have any furniture you'll need to set up some areas of security for him such as towel-lined boxes that he can hide in. Put a couple of boxes in the closet too. Bring in a chair or some other furniture for him to hide under. And put a scratching post in there for him.

If you don't have one already, get a cat carrier, line it with a towel, and leave it open in the room. This is so he'll begin to get used to it.

He'll eventually use it to sleep in. That way you'll start alleviating that fear he'll have whenever you bring the carrier out for transporting the cat to the vet (especially if he has injuries that need regular monitoring). But for right now, the carrier will serve as an extra hiding place.

Your immediate objective for this cat is to establish that the environment he's in is secure and safe. Put a bowl of water down for him. Spike the water with a few drops of the Rescue Remedy (see Chapter 3). The Rescue Remedy may ease the initial panic and shock of the situation and help him accept the comfort and security you're offering.

If you have an ionizer, set it up in the room. If the cat won't come out from under the bed or chair then leave a bowl of food out for him. Bring a few articles of clothing with your scent into the room and leave them on the floor so the cat can become familiar with you. You can also use the scented clothing to line his bed. Once you've done this, leave the room if he doesn't want your comfort and chooses to hide. He's overwhelmed and needs to get his bearings. With you out of the room he'll be able to check out his surroundings and hopefully eat some of the meal you've prepared.

In the beginning, limit your contact with him to short periods of time. Don't seek him out or try to hold him (unless of course he's asking for you by seeking you out for comfort). Let him control the pace of everything. You may only be able to have voice contact with him. When you do talk to him, keep your tone quiet and soothing.

As he becomes more comfortable, put the food bowl closer to you. It may take a few weeks for him to get to the point where he'll even eat with you in the room, so don't be discouraged.

Let the cat come up and make the initial physical contact with you before you attempt to reach out and pet him. I usually bring a book in the room with me and sit on the floor and read. This way I remain relaxed and casual and the cat can check me out unobserved. When he seems a little more relaxed, I read aloud quietly to help him get used to my voice. For reading aloud I often keep a few children's books on hand. The tone of voice you naturally use for reading to a child is perfect for a frightened cat. Treat it as if you're reading a bedtime story to your children. You'll speak in a quiet, soothing way. (Not at all the way you'd read aloud if you had a Stephen King suspense novel.) I know it may seem a bit silly to be reading a bedtime story to a cat, but it works. You don't have to spend an hour reading Mother Goose. Bring in another book to read to yourself, then take a break and read the children's book for a few minutes. When reading, turn the pages quietly to avoid frightening the cat just as he gets close to you. I sometimes leave a little catnip out on a paper plate near me as I read. Once the cat is no longer showing so much fear, you can begin to use the Kitty Tease to play gently with him.

Always make your movements slowly and quietly because they'll appear magnified to a frightened cat. Get down on his level and let him investigate you. Then, when you feel the time is right, you can begin to let him get acquainted with other family members. You can start by bringing in scented clothing before actually introducing the person. Go slowly, making sure the cat gets used to one person at a time. Children will need specific instructions on how to move slowly and quietly around the new kitty. Each person will have to go through the same routine you did in terms of letting the cat initiate contact.

As things progress successfully you can begin to leave the door open a bit so the kitty can peek out if he chooses. In time, he'll feel comfortable to venture out. Be patient because in some cases it can take months to get to this point. When he does begin to come out, family members need to adjust their pace within the home a bit. Walking will have to be done a little quieter (and no running), speaking will have to be in a more soothing tone, and sudden noises are to be avoided. Remember, you're dealing with a traumatized cat who needs the constant reassurance that you're providing a completely safe and comforting atmosphere.

If you have other cats in the house, your new cat may have trouble socializing. Consider temporarily installing a screen door to his room so everyone can begin to have safe contact with each other.

Since your new cat is very sensitive and carries who knows how many emotional scars with him from his previous life, he needs lots of positives now. Even though he probably won't have the best manners at first, refrain from reprimanding him for mistakes. Use positive reinforcement and the behavior modification techniques described in this book to help him distinguish the good behavior from the undesirable behavior. Winning over an abused or neglected cat can take anywhere from a few weeks to a few years. Your best tools are love, support, and patience. The payoff can be spectacular as you watch your cat begin to see the joy in life for the first time.

If the cat is extremely aggressive, refer to Chapter 8. You can try dissolving a "Calms" tablet into his food. These tablets are available at natural food stores. In some cases, your vet may need to prescribe a mild tranquilizer. If that happens, you'll really have to combine it with behavior modification so that the aggression won't return when the medication is stopped.

Since a cat who has been traumatized in the past probably won't handle such things as being loaded into a carrier and driven to the vet without kicking and screaming, help him make a smooth adjustment. Get him used to being enclosed in the carrier and tolerating car travel by following the directions in Chapter 16.

chapter 15

The Elderly Cat

Although she may still look like the same cat you've always known, advancing age causes changes in the cat's mind and body. This is the time in your cat's life when all your years of good care, top quality nutrition, veterinary checkups, regular exercise, grooming, and most of all, love, can really pay off. Though all these things are no guarantee that a cat will live to be fifteen or twenty years old, her environment has a definite influence on the aging process. A cat kept fit with proper nutrition and exercise, living in an environment that provides the right amount of stimulation and a minimal amount of stress stands a greater chance of enjoying more of her golden years than a cat who has been viewed as a "low maintenance" pet by her owners.

Of course, even with the best care, sometimes you just can't fight off certain diseases. I've watched cats who have had the very best care still succumb to unbeatable conditions. We can take some comfort in knowing that all the good care made our cats stronger and perhaps gave them more years before the disease could grab hold.

As cats age, they experience a decline in their senses. By being aware of this fact, you can help your cat make an easier adjustment.

Hearing

Avoid startling your cat. Come into her field of vision before picking her up or touching her. You can also knock on the floor next to her to get her attention because she'll be able to feel the vibration.

Sight

If your cat is losing her vision, keep furniture in the same location. Since vision declines gradually, animals are able to adjust rather well, provided you don't rearrange the furniture. If you're planning to redecorate, do it gradually—one piece at a time to allow your cat adequate time to adjust. Help her learn the location of the new piece of furniture.

Smell and Taste

The way food smells has a big influence over a cat's desire to eat. As her sense of smell begins to fail, her appetite will most likely decline. You can certainly relate to that if you've ever had a horrible head cold and had to force yourself to eat. You can spark your cat's appetite by warming her food to release more of the aroma. You can also try adding some chopped fresh garlic and brewer's yeast powder (both of which have a strong smell and taste) to the food. If your cat still refuses to eat, contact your veterinarian for his or her recommendation. Don't start adding all kinds of treat foods because now isn't the time to start overworking the cat's kidneys or digestive system. Your vet will have a recommendation based upon your cat's specific medical condition.

Touch

Due to arthritis, increased sensitivity, or other condition, you may need to adjust how you pet and handle your cat. If she has lost weight, she'll have more boney protrusions so you'll have to be very gentle with her grooming. You may need to replace the brush you normally use with a much softer one. Petting your cat should now include a search with your fingers for any lumps or growths that may need to be looked at by your vet.

Here are more suggestions to help your cat both mentally and physically adjust to life as a senior citizen.

- An aging cat may not be as fastidious about personal hygiene as she used to be in her youth. Help her stay clean with regular brushing. Pay particular attention to keeping the facial area and around the genitals clean.

- Elderly cats love to snooze in the sun so provide a comfortable spot near a sunny window.
- Keep your cat away from drafts.
- Be tolerant of an old cat's litter box habits. She may miss the box occasionally. If walking is difficult or if she can't always make it to the box in time, provide several boxes for her. You may even have to help her to the litter box. Use low-sided litter boxes without covers.
- Provide your cat with continued top quality nutrition. If your vet has her on a prescription diet for a medical condition then be faithful to it and don't sneak treats. To ease the work load on her digestive system, your vet may also recommend feeding smaller meals more frequently.
- Use only spring or distilled water.
- Have your cat examined by the vet every six months.
- If your cat used to love jumping up to a particular spot but now has difficulty, provide her with some steps or a ramp so she can enjoy her favorite places. The PawsWay ramp is available by mail order. It will enable your cat to get on and off sofas and beds. The carpeted ramp is adjustable (16 inches maximum) and can be folded. Check the Appendix for the address. To allow your cat access to counters or favorite windows you may want to consider constructing a small set of portable type stairs.
- Monitor your cat's weight and food/water intake. Inform your vet of any changes. (For example, increased water consumption could be a symptom of kidney failure or diabetes.)
- Continue a schedule of regular grooming. Also use this time to do a home health exam to check the skin, teeth and gums, eyes, ears, any lumps or growths, coat condition, etc.
- Some older cats enjoy a gentle massage, especially if they experience stiffness. To learn the proper massage technique, I recommend you read *The Healing Touch*, by Dr. Michael Fox (Newmarket Press). Please check with your vet first.
- You may find your older cat seeking you out more than she used to in the past. Now's the time to let her curl up on your lap and feel the comfort and security you provide.
- You may discover your cat has started calling out (especially at night). This may happen due to decreased hearing or she may be a little disoriented. Usually calling out or letting her see you will quiet her.

chapter 16

Questions Cat Owners Ask

My cat is very sweet and gentle at home but becomes defensive and angry whenever I have to take her to someone else's home. She'll even hiss at me and lash out. Any suggestions?

Your cat's anger and defensive behavior is triggered by fear. Since cats are territorial, removing her from the familiar territory and placing her in strange surroundings is too overwhelming. The reason she's so sweet and gentle in her own home is because she feels secure and not threatened. In someone else's home she's very intimidated and doesn't know what dangers await her.

If you must bring her along to someone else's home, set her up in a quiet room with her litter box, bed, water and toys. Bringing along an article of clothing with your scent on it can also be very comforting for her while in unfamiliar territory.

Give her time to become adjusted and don't have people coming in to see her while she's making an adjustment. Don't force her to be sociable while she's under stress. After she becomes comfortable you can allow a visitor in to say hello.

Even though your cat may not show much interest in her food at this time, continue her diet of good nutrition. Don't weaken and offer all kinds of treats. Her stomach is nervous and needs the familiarity of her own food.

Sprinkling a little catnip in the room for her can also be a great stress reliever.

• *How can I keep my cat from jumping on the kitchen counter?*

Cats love high places. Not only do they allow a better view of the cat's surroundings, they also provide a sense of security. A cat who chooses to recline on top of your counter feels less vulnerable during this relaxed time. On the other hand, there's the curious side of the cat, and food-filled kitchen counters can be too tempting to resist.

The most important aspect of training a cat where he is and isn't permitted is consistency. Don't confuse your cat by allowing him on the dining room table as long as there's no food there. Decide which places he's allowed to jump on and don't compromise.

The best way to train a cat to stay off the counter is to make that particular spot unpleasant. Collect empty soda cans, put several pennies in each and tape over the openings (use only empty cans to avoid injury to the cat). Take these cans and set them up along the edge of the counter or table, a few inches apart. This way, when the cat jumps up he'll knock over the cans. The sound they make as they hit the floor will be very unpleasant to the cat. Now, you'll have to be patient because it may take several attempts before he finally gets the message. Every time he knocks the cans down you set them back up. This form of training will condition the cat to believe the counter isn't a fun place and the training will remain effective even after the soda cans are no longer there. It also helps that the cat is coming to this conclusion by himself and not connecting the "negative training" directly with you, his loving owner.

When you're in the kitchen working and he jumps on the counter have your trusty squirt bottle handy and give him a quick spritz with plain water.

Another method that's been used is to put double-faced tape on the counters. The cat will truly dislike walking on the surface.

Since cats do enjoy high places, make sure you've given him a few spots that are acceptable. You can even get him his own cat tree so he'll have a place that's just his. Make one yourself or, if you prefer, there are several companies that make interesting looking trees. Cat House Originals makes a tall tree that you can have customized. Their address is in the Appendix.

• *I allow my cat to walk and sit on my countertops, provided I'm not preparing food. Someone said I could get toxoplasmosis. Is it really a health hazard to let him jump on the counter?*

Cat owners will always disagree on this. The main worry people have when it comes to allowing cats to walk on the same surfaces we use for food preparation is toxoplasmosis. The eggs of this parasite are passed out in the feces of an infected cat. Toxoplasmosis is of particular danger for pregnant women who can pass the disease along to the fetus. Not every cat carries the parasite. Many people and cats carry this disease and then develop an immunity. You're at more of a risk of contracting toxoplasmosis by touching raw meat and then touching vegetables that will be eaten raw (such as salad) without first washing your hands. Also, using a cutting surface to prepare meat and then using the same surface to prepare vegetables is another potential danger.

Keep all work surfaces clean and always wash your hands after handling raw meat or changing the litter box and you'll greatly reduce your chance of ever coming in contact with toxoplasmosis. For more on Toxoplasmosis refer to Chapter 12.

If your cat is going to be allowed on the counter, the one place he must never be allowed on is the stove. No matter if the heat is off and the stove is cold, he should be forbidden to jump up there. Too many cats have jumped up and knocked a hot pan over and been burned or else they've jumped up while the burners are still warm. Use a plant sprayer (with plain water) if you have to, but make sure he knows this is one spot that's always off limits.

• *My kitten bites and scratches me whenever I try to trim his nails. What should I do?*

The best way to train a kitten to cooperate during nail trimming is to get him used to it in gradual steps. First, don't attempt to do it when your cat is revved up and ready to play. He'll only view what you're trying to do as a big game.

To accustom a kitten to nail trimming requires you to first get him used to having his paws touched. Most cats hate having anything done to their paws. When your kitten is quiet and sleepy, gently pet him, paying particular attention to stroking his paws. When he's comfortable having them stroked you can gently hold a paw in your hand (only for a few seconds) and then release. Gently pick up another paw and hold it for a few seconds. All the time this is being done be sure to praise your cat and talk to him reassuringly.

The next step is to hold a paw in your hand and gently press to extend the nails. Do this carefully and quickly so your cat won't become alarmed. As you're able to extend your cat's nails without his objection, take a good look at the nails themselves. Notice where the "pink" starts: this is where the nerve endings are and the blood supply is. You'll need to be very careful that you never clip too much of the nail. You never want to clip that part of the nail because you'll cause pain to your cat and the nail will bleed. Also, it'll make him very reluctant to have his nails trimmed again. So only clip the very tip of the nail—don't go beyond the curve.

Use nail trimmers meant for cats or you can use the kind of trimmers you use on your own nails. Don't use dog nail trimmers because they're too big and you risk cutting too much.

In the beginning don't attempt to do all the nails in one sitting. If you can only do half, then do the others at another quiet time. If you make the experience painless, casual, and quick, your cat won't object and you'll eventually be able to do all the nails in less than a minute. Don't yank your cat's leg, yell at him, or ever give him a reason to view nail trimming as a punishment.

Always praise your kitten or cat after the nail trimming and provide a treat (a healthy one like a brewer's yeast tablet). Don't be insulted if your cat runs right over to the scratching post after a pedicure.

- *Can I teach my cat to walk on a leash?*

Cats can be leash trained but it takes time and patience to get him used to the procedure. Leash training can be a safe way to allow your cat to enjoy the benefits of the outdoors.

Some things to consider before leash training are 1) your cat's temperament and 2) the area in which you live. If your cat is very nervous and sensitive, the sounds, sights, and smells of the outdoors can be too overwhelming. If your cat is very territorial, then exposing him to the outdoors and increasing the amount of territory he has to worry about can make the situation worse. Make sure the cat you want to leash train is even-tempered and not easily frightened by noises. Your other consideration is your location. No matter how even-tempered your cat is, you don't need to be walking him down a busy street with children riding by on bicycles, cars whizzing by, dogs barking, lawn mowers roaring, etc. The walk won't be enjoyable and certainly won't be safe for your cat. Only walk your cat in quiet areas where he can enjoy the normal sounds of nature. The safety of your own back-yard is as far as he needs to go.

Training your cat to the leash involves various stages. Don't rush it or else your cat will be conditioned to dislike the process. Step one is to get a harness made especially for cats (a Figure 8 harness). You can find one at the pet supply store. Don't use a collar because I promise you that your cat will be able to pull out of it and you also risk injuring your cat's neck. Don't get a dog harness either because it won't fit your cat properly. Take the Figure 8 harness and lay it on the floor so your cat can investigate it. Let it remain there for a day or two.

The next step is to gently place the cat in the harness and let him adjust to wearing it. He'll probably work frantically to get out of it but

that's okay. Use distraction such as playing with the Cat Dancer or offering catnip to take your cat's mind off this strange contraption he has suddenly found himself in. You can also put the harness on the cat before dinner and then offer him his meal. Put the harness on your cat for about ten minutes three or four times a day. Don't leave him alone, though, during this time; always supervise. You want to get to the point where he'll accept the harness and not even realize he's wearing it.

Now it's time for the leash. Use a lightweight nylon leash and attach it to the harness. Let your cat drag it around. Don't hold it in your hand yet. Right now you just want him to get used to the idea of having this extra piece of equipment around. When he's comfortable with that, you'll take the leash in your hand. Don't tug or pull. Let him go where he wants. Talk to your cat reassuringly. Have some brewer's yeast tablets in your pocket to use as treats. Walk a few steps in front of your cat and then hold a treat a little in front of him at his eye level. When he walks to it, reward him. This is how you teach him to walk with you and to accept the gentle tug of the leash. Keep repeating the process and each time give the leash a gentle tug.

Make sure he sees the treat and always reward him when he comes to you. Eventually you'll eliminate the treat (but always continue the praise) as he gets comfortable with walking in the direction you want.

Practice walking him on a leash indoors for several weeks before attempting to go outdoors. He needs to be totally comfortable with the harness and leash before going outside. The last thing you want is for him to be desperately trying to free himself while you're outdoors.

When you feel he's ready for the outdoors, make sure you have an identification tag on your cat's harness that states he's an indoor cat. Include your name and phone number. This is vital should the unforeseen happen and he gets away from you.

When you go outside always carry him out. Don't let him walk out the door. You don't want to be training him that he can just run outside any time he sees the door open. So carry him each and every time. The first time you go out you should keep him in your arms for a while as he adjusts to the new surroundings. Stay close to the house, maybe even right outside the door at first.

Although you may be hoping to provide your cat with exercise by enjoying a brisk walk in the yard, you have to realize that's probably not going to happen. Cats are different than dogs and you can't expect him to go trotting along at your pace. Your cat is inquisitive and he'll want to stop and sniff every flower, every rock, and nearly every single blade of grass. He'll also get distracted by birds, bugs, squirrels or anything else that happens by. Let him enjoy the outdoors at his pace in his own way.

When you have your cat outside on a leash you need to be constantly aware of everything around you. The sudden appearance of another cat, a dog or even a bird can send your cat into a panic or cause him to dart off after something. Always keep a firm hold on the leash with the loop around your wrist. Be ready to scoop him up in the event of an emergency.

Another thing to be aware of when you take your cat outside is that he's now going to be exposed to things that he hadn't been previously, such as fleas, ticks, etc. During flea and tick season you need to check him over after each outing so you don't bring any little parasites into the house. Also, have your cat up-to-date on all his vaccinations before going outdoors.

• *My cat wakes me up at 6:00 a.m. every morning for her breakfast. What can I do to stop this behavior?*

Very often, when a cat starts meowing incessantly or pawing at you to get out of bed, there seems to be no other way to quiet her but to get up and toss food in her bowl.

She happily munches away and you go back to bed knowing you won't be disturbed anymore...that is, until tomorrow morning at 6:00 a.m. when the whole thing starts all over again.

Unfortunately, the very thing you're doing to keep her quiet is the thing that's reinforcing the undesirable behavior. By getting up and feeding her you're rewarding her actions. A cat is a very smart creature and she quickly learns what works and what doesn't. Each cat will have a slight variation in technique but the effect is the same. Some owners tell me how their cats sit on the bed and stare at them. Some cats meow and others paw to get attention. There are even some who jump up on the night table and systematically push things to the floor, such as coins or jewelry. You may even have been the recipient of a good morning bite on the toe.

No matter what technique your cat uses, you have to stop rewarding her with what she wants. You need to ignore her until you're ready to get up. Brace yourself because I'll tell you right now, it's going to be very tough. At first she's not going to understand why you're no longer responding the way you should. Hang in there, though, and eventually she'll get the message.

If she makes it impossible to ignore her by biting, scratching, or meowing so loud you can't stand it, then close her out of your bedroom.

When you do finally get out of bed don't feed her right away. Pet her and tell her what a good cat she is. Then do a couple of quick things like combing your hair or making the bed. Then you can feed her. The reason I don't want you to feed her right away is that I don't want her to make the direct connection with you getting out of bed and her getting breakfast. This way she'll know there are a couple of steps in between and she'll adjust her schedule.

Not every cat wakes the owner up for breakfast. Some just want to play. After all, you've been asleep for eight hours and she's had no one to play with. There are many cats who don't even wait until morning— they pounce on you in the middle of the night. If your cat is asking to play while you're still in bed, you can easily adjust her schedule to coincide with yours. Very often, serving her dinner a little later in the evening helps. Also, add a Play Therapy session at night, right before you go to bed. This step is important because she'll be more inclined to sleep through the night and less likely to go in search of adventure. The Play Therapy session should last about fifteen minutes so she'll be left satisfied when it's over. You don't want to leave her all excited, so make sure you've spent enough playtime with her.

Leaving some fun things out at night can help a restless kitty. Place an open paper bag on the floor with a toy in it or perhaps a couple of boxes can be left out. Rotate toys to avoid boredom and if your cat is an only child, consider adopting a companion cat.

- *Can you teach a cat to come when you call his name?*

Yes. Begin by softly repeating his name every time you pet him. He'll begin to associate the name with the nice way he feels while being stroked. Also, call his name every time you prepare his dinner. Again, he'll be learning to associate the name with something good.

After you've done the groundwork by having him associate his name with good things, have a treat in your hand (such as a brewer's yeast tablet) and call your cat. Use the same positive tone that you used when you were preparing his dinner. Don't try calling him when he's sound asleep or concentrating on a bird that's just outside the window. Call him when he's looking at you. When he comes, reward him with the treat. Don't keep repeating the game. You can try again later. Make it seem like you have a reason to call him.

During training, always be ready with a treat to reward him and continue to say his name during pleasurable things such as stroking and petting. Eventually you'll be able to call him from another room.

After solid training, when his name has been firmly established in his head you can taper off on the food rewards but always praise him when he comes to you.

Never call a cat to you to punish him for something. He'll eventually learn to not respond to his name if he knows he's going to get in trouble. And, always, when you call his name use a positive and loving tone.

If you have many cute and loving nicknames for your cat, refrain from using them when you're trying to get your cat to come when called. He can't be expected to respond to several names. Use one name and stick with that. It also helps if the name is relatively simple and easily recognized.

- *Is there any way to stop the neighborhood cats from using my garden as a litter box?*

This is a tough one. My first answer is if you know who the owners are, try talking to them and explaining the situation. Perhaps they would agree to keep their cats indoors. Of course, I realize that very often you don't know who the cats belong to and even if you did, it can be very touchy when you attempt to ask owners to confine their cats. So your best defense is to make your garden unappealing to the cats.

First let's talk about what not to do. Many people have tried using cat repellent sprays but they never seem to work. Others have tried placing citrus rinds in the garden because cats generally dislike that scent. I advise against this, though, because the citrus rinds will only attract other critters to your yard (such as raccoons). Another method gardeners have used is placing mothballs around the garden. This is an extremely dangerous thing to do. Mothballs are highly toxic to cats. The fumes alone will damage a cat's liver in a very short time. If you've been using mothballs, remove them immediately.

Now, for the correct method. Since cats like to first dig in the garden before they eliminate, spread some netting down (available at garden centers) around the plants. You can sprinkle a light layer of soil over the netting. Add stability to the netting by placing some large rocks around to hold it in place. Arrange the rocks so they look decorative and no one will know what their actual purpose is. If you don't want to use rocks you can secure the netting with some stakes. This way, when the cat goes to dig in the soil his claws will catch on the netting. He'll get the idea quickly and will go in search of a better spot.

When working in a garden frequented by cats, be sure to wear gardening gloves and wash your hands immediately afterwards to prevent the chance of getting toxoplasmosis. This parasite can be transmitted to humans from contaminated cat feces.

• *Why does my cat start talking and making funny noises whenever she spots a bird while looking out the window?*

The "talking" you hear is the result of her excitement. To see a bird outside is a very exciting experience and her enthusiasm causes her to start chirping and chattering. This is common behavior among cats.

• *I want my outdoor cat to have identification but he hates wearing his collar. How can I get him to accept it?*

Let him become acquainted with the collar itself before you attempt to put it on. Rub a little catnip on it and toss it on the floor. Leave the collar on the floor for a few days. When you first put the collar on your cat have an interactive toy handy (like the Cat Dancer or the Kitty Tease) so you can immediately distract him with playtime. Plan this out so it's scheduled before mealtime. Feeding him some dinner will then further distract him from the collar.

Don't put a dangling ID tag or bell on the collar until your cat is totally comfortable with wearing the collar. Then, the first few times you put the collar with the tag on, use playtime as a distraction.

If you're going to have your cat wear a collar be sure it's a breakaway collar. Then, if the cat gets hung up on a tree branch or fence he won't strangle himself. Even if you put a collar on an indoor cat it should be a breakaway collar.

• *My twelve-year-old cat has started howling. She used to do it only at night but now she howls during the day, too. What causes that?*

Make an appointment to see your vet to be sure that the howling isn't the result of a more serious medical condition.

Cats howl for many reasons. In older cats, as hearing and eyesight diminish they might begin to howl. Sometimes a disoriented cat will howl. A cat who thinks she's alone in the house may also howl.

If your older cat appears to be howling because she's disoriented, let her see you or at least call out to comfort her. This also works with a cat who thinks she's alone in the house. Sometimes just calling her name is enough. For an older cat with diminished hearing or eyesight, provide as much physical comfort as possible.

Howling can also be helped by the addition of a companion cat. It can be comforting for an older cat and wonderful companionship for a lonely cat.

• *Whenever my two cats groom each other it always ends with someone getting bitten on the neck. Are they fighting or playing?*

The neck bite is a carry-over behavior from the mating ritual. Grooming is a very pleasurable, emotional experience and some cats respond to that sensual feeling.

• *My cat needs a bath every now and then because of fleas but he becomes so uncontrollable and violent. I bathe him in the sink with the spray attachment. How can I get him to accept being bathed?*

The force of the spray attachment makes a sound that can be very frightening to a kitty. Hook up a hose or use a spray attachment with the sprayer cut off. This way the water will run out of the hose quietly and won't be so alarming.

Have all of your bathing equipment ready before you get the cat. Make sure the room is warm. Put a bath mat in the sink or tub to provide a secure gripping surface for a frightened cat.

Be certain to maintain a calm, peaceful attitude when it comes to bath time. Your cat will pick up on any nervousness you convey. One thing that often helps me is to play some soft music during bath time. I also talk reassuringly to the cat during the entire procedure. I tell him what a good kitty he is and how this bath will make him feel so much better.

Put a piece of cotton in each ear so water doesn't get in there and use a gentle shampoo meant for cats. Don't use too much shampoo or you'll be endlessly rinsing to get the shampoo out. Make sure you get every trace of soap off the cat or you'll end up irritating his skin.

Wrap your cat in an absorbent towel. Have several handy so you can absorb as much water as possible. Then use a hair dryer on a low setting. It really does pay to buy a hair dryer that's extra quiet. If your cat absolutely refuses to tolerate a dryer of any kind then put him in his carrier or a small room until he's dried. You don't want him running all over the house while he's wet because he'll become a magnet for every piece of dust in his path.

Praise your cat after a bath and reward him with a treat.

• *My cat grooms herself excessively, almost to the point of licking all the fur off her hind legs. We recently moved to a new home which she seems to like so what can be causing the problem?*

Even though your cat may seem to be adjusting to the new house, a move is still a very stressful experience. Her stress began as you were preparing for the move (all the boxes being packed and furniture being moved). Then, the territory she was used to was replaced by unfamiliar surroundings. Everyone around her has probably been in a more excitable state as they packed and unpacked boxes and began their own adjustment to the house. Your cat might even be spotting a strange cat outside causing her to become nervous and feel threatened.

First, have your cat examined by the vet to rule out any medical cause for the excessive grooming. Once she gets a clean bill of health your job will be to help ease her adjustment to her new home. Start by making sure she's on a top quality diet. If you haven't been feeding a premium quality food then make the changeover gradual so you aren't causing her more stress. Add a little of the new food in with the old food. Once she has accepted this then increase the amount of new food while decreasing the amount of old food. Adding the dry mix discussed in Chapter 5 may also help her. I would also mix one-quarter teaspoon chamomile tea leaves into her food. Chamomile has a calming effect and is safe and natural. Your vet may also recommend a prescription diet such as Hill's Prescription Diet Feline d/d or Wysong Anergen.

If your cat has licked her fur down to the skin, or if the skin has become red and irritated, use Natural Animal's Spritz Coat Enhancer (see Appendix for address). Spritz has a soothing effect and will help improve the condition of the hair. If your cat has a flea problem you can also spray the Spritz Coat Enhancer over her coat and it will relieve the irritation caused by flea bites.

If you haven't been using an ionizer in your home now would be the time to get one. The next step is Play Therapy and your cat is one who'll truly benefit from this. Incorporate at least two Play Therapy sessions a day, fifteen minutes in the morning and fifteen minutes at night. If there's someone home during the middle part of the day it would be good to add a Play Therapy session then also. For specifics on Play Therapy refer to Chapter 4. For more help with handling stress and nervousness, refer to Chapter 9.

• *I have to take my cat to the vet for his annual vaccinations but it's always a horrible battle to get him into his carrier. Then, on the ride over he screams the entire time. How can I get him to the vet without such a fight?*

If the only time your cat sees the carrier come out is when he's going to the vet, I'm afraid you'll always have a battle on your hands. The same holds true for the car. If the only time he rides in the car is when going to the vet then you might as well buy yourself some ear plugs because he's not going to stop screaming. To change the behavior you'll need to go back to the beginning and reintroduce your cat to the carrier to allow him to view it in a different light.

The first step in the reintroduction is to leave the carrier out all the time. No matter what kind of carrier you have, set it up so it can be used as a cozy bed for your cat. Line it with a towel and put it in a corner where your cat might enjoy napping. Your cat probably won't go into it right away; in fact, when you first set it up he's more than likely going to run for cover. Eventually, he'll peek his little nose out from under the bed, then slink back out, totally confused as to why you're not trying to snatch him up and whisk him off to that dreaded place where he gets stuck with needles.

When your cat is using the carrier to nap in and is very comfortable going in and out of it you can casually close the door halfway (so he can easily push it open to get out). The next step is to close it completely but only for a second or two and then open it back up. Talk in soothing tones to your cat, praising him for taking this so beautifully.

When your cat has completely accepted all the steps so far, the next phase is to close the door, lift the carrier off the ground, walk across the room and then back again. Open the door and have a treat ready for your kitty as a reward. You can practice this every once in a while, increasing the amount of time he's in the carrier—for instance, walk through the house and back. Don't do this every time your cat goes in the carrier because you want him to still view it as a cozy napping place. He won't do that if he gets disturbed every single time he goes in there.

Not every cat will use his carrier as a bed but by keeping it out you'll take his fear away. That can be important in an emergency because if you had to grab your cat and get out of the house (in the case of a fire, for instance), you'll know right where to find the carrier and you won't have so much trouble getting your cat into it. To help your cat adjust to car travel, take him for short rides (always in his carrier) around the block and back. Always finish with much praise and a reward (such as a brewer's yeast tablet or maybe a little catnip party). Gradually increase the distance each time. It may also help your cat if you drive to the vet and bring him in just for some petting and a treat by one of the vet's staff.

• *Due to cancer, my cat is going blind. He has always been an indoor cat. Do I need to confine him to one room? How will he know where his litter box is?*

If you've been keeping his litter box in the same location he'll probably have little trouble remembering where it is. As long as you don't rearrange the furniture, your cat will negotiate his environment based on his memory, with help from his ears, nose, and whiskers. That's why it's important to avoid disorienting him by adding, subtracting, or rearranging furniture.

That same memory will enable your cat to locate his food and water also. A word of caution: If your cat used to have his meals served on a counter or other elevated spot, you should begin feeding him on the floor now. It would be too dangerous for him to attempt jumping.

Blind cats can be startled easily so always announce your intentions to touch/pet or pick him up by talking to him first. This will avoid the problem of a startled cat biting at a sudden, unexpected touch.

Talk to your cat often to help ease his feeling of isolation. This will help increase his feeling of security. If he enjoys petting or brushing, indulge him in several sessions of comforting touch.

When you leave for work, turn on the radio. And, if you're going out of town and are having someone come in to feed your cat, make sure it's someone he already knows and trusts. Instruct your pet sitter to talk to your cat and announce his or her intentions before touching.

Since a cat without sight may tend to become less active, you'll have to find ways to adapt his favorite games to enable him to still enjoy playtime. Family members, and especially children, need to be more aware of their actions so they don't accidentally step on the cat or bump into him. Any visitors to the house will also need to be made aware that your cat is blind.

And of course you know that a blind cat must never have access to the outdoors. With some adjustments on your part to help accommodate your cat's disability, he will still be the same loving companion as before.

suggested reading list

The Bach Flower Remedies, by Edward Bach, M.D., and F.J. Wheeler, M.D. Keats, New Canaan, CT, 1977

Bach Flower Remedies to the Rescue, by Gregory Vlamis. Healing Arts Press, Rochester, VT, 1988

The Bach Flower Remedies Step By Step, by Judy Howard. C.W. Daniel Company Ltd., Saffron Walden, Essex, England, 1990

Questions & Answers: Explaining the Basic Principles and Standards of the Bach Flower Remedies, by John Ramsell. C.W. Daniel Company Ltd., Saffron Walden, Essex, England, 1986, 1991

The Body Language and Emotion of Cats, by Myrna M. Milani, D.V.M. William Morrow & Company, New York, NY, 1987

A Cat Is Watching, by Roger A. Caras. Simon and Schuster, New York, NY, 1989

The Healing Touch, by Dr. Michael W. Fox. Newmarket Press, New York, NY, 1983

The Tellington TTouch: A Breakthrough Technique to Train and Care for Your Favorite Animal, by Linda Tellington-Jones with Sybil Taylor. Viking Press, New York, NY, 1992

appendix

Cat Foods And Supplements:

Hill's Pet Products
P.O. Box 148
Topeka, KS 66601
1-800-445-5777 (customer affairs)
Makers of Science Diet and the Prescription line of pet foods.

Natural Life Pet Products
1601 West McKay
Frontenac, KS 66763
1-800-367-2391
Manufacturer of natural pet foods. Sold in pet supply stores.

Nature's Recipe
341 Bonnie Circle
Corona, CA 91720
1-800-843-4008
Manufacturer of natural pet foods. Sold in natural food stores.

PetGuard, Inc.
P.O. Box 728
Orange Park, FL 32073
1-800-874-3221
Manufacturer of natural pet foods and other products. Sold in
natural food stores or you can call them for a catalog.

The Iams Company
7250 Poe Avenue
Dayton, OH 45414
1-800-525-4267
Manufacturer of Iams Cat Food.

Very Healthy Enterprises Inc.
P.O. Box 4489
Inglewood, CA 90309
1-800-222-9932
Suppliers of Feline Digestive Enzyme Powder.

Wysong Medical Corporation
1880 North Eastman Road
Midland, MI 48640
Manufacturer of natural pet food formulas. They also make the
Diagnostic Litter, Diagnostic Pads, and Litter Lite. Write for a
catalog.

Cat Products and Mail Order Companies

Cat House Originals
P.O. Box 61
1059 Colora Road
Colora, MD 21917-0061
1-410-658-CATS
Custom designed cat trees. Call or write for information and they'll
send sketches of the different components so you can choose what
you'd like. The tree will arrive fully assembled.

Drs. Foster & Smith Inc.
2253 Air Park Road
P.O. Box 100
Rhinelander, WI 54501-0100
1-800-826-7206
My favorite mail order company. They carry Nature's Miracle, A-
frame beds, grooming supplies, brewer's yeast tablets, leashes, and
lots of pet care necessities. Run by two veterinarians, this company
is unique in that they provide a service whereby you can speak to a
veterinarian at no charge if you have a question on general care or
how to use any of the products. The catalog is set up with lots of
helpful information on pet care and disease prevention.

Eco Safe Products
P.O. Box 1177
St. Augustine, FL 32085
1-800-274-7387
Manufacturer of Natural Animal's Spritz Coat Enhancer. There is a
formula for cats and also one for dogs.

Felix Company
3623 Fremont Avenue N.
Seattle, WA 98103
1-800-24-FELIX
Supplier of the Felix Katnip Tree scratching post. Worth the money!
They also sell wonderful loose catnip.

Galkie Company
P.O. Box 20
Harrogate, TN 37752
1-615-869-8138
Maker of the Kitty Tease. You can order it by mail. They even sell
replacement line in case your cat chews through it. The Kitty Tease
comes in two sizes—the regular and a great little travel size.

Go Cat
3248 Mulliken Road
Charlotte, MI 48813
1-517-543-7519
Manufacturer of Da Bird. Every cat needs one. Available at pet
supply stores.

Hobar Manufacturing Inc.
30 Huntoon Memorial Highway
Leicester, MA 01524-1266
Manufacturer of a good quality cat window shelf. You can write for a
catalog.

Neo-Life Company of America
3500 Gateway Blvd.
Fremont, CA 94538
Makers of a wonderful ionizer called the Consolaire. They also make
great vitamins, supplements, and a water filtering system. If there's
no local distributor listed in your phone book, write to Neo-Life for
the name of one nearest your location.

Pet Care With Love Inc.
P.O. Box 764
Glenview, IL 60025-0764
They make the PawsWay ramp. It's available in pine or oak and is
covered in a stain-resistant carpet. The ramp is adjustable to four
different heights (for a maximum of sixteen inches).

Pets 'n People, Inc.
930 Indian Peak Road
Suite 215
Rolling Hills Estates, CA 90274
1-310-544-7125
Manufacturer of Nature's Miracle. If you have any questions on how
to handle a particular stain or odor problem with Nature's Miracle,
give them a call.

The Mail Shop
111 E. Canal Street
Neenah, WI 54956
Makers of the Cat Dancer. This toy should be widely available at pet supply stores. If not, tell your local store to order it.

Yesterday's News
2700 Matheson Blvd., East
Mississauga, Ontario L4W 4V9 (Canada)
1-617-592-3373 (USA)
Makers of Yesterday's News, a cat litter made from pelletized newspaper. Ask your vet or local pet supply store to stock it.

Magazines:

Cat Fancy
Subscription Department
P.O. Box 52864
Boulder, CO 80322-2864
1-303-786-7306

Cats
Subscription Department
P.O. Box 420240
Palm Coast, FL 32142-0240
1-800-829-9125

I Love Cats
Subscription Department
 950 Third Avenue
New York, NY 10022-2705
1-212-888-1855

Tiger Tribe
1407 East College Street
Iowa City, Iowa 52245-4410
1-319-351-6698
1-319-354-8296 (FAX)
A magazine dedicated to holistic health care for cats.

Additional Information:

American Holistic Veterinary Association
2214 Old Eramorton Road
Bel Air, MD 21014
If you're interested in learning more about alternative techniques used in veterinary medicine (the use of homeopathy, nutrition, acupuncture, herbs, Bach Flowers), send a stamped, self-addressed envelope for a list of holistic veterinarians closest to your location.

Feline Health Center
Cornell University
College of Veterinary Medicine
Ithaca, NY 14853
1-800-548-8937
A phone consultation with a veterinarian is available for a $25 fee.

index

RELATED BOOKS BY THE CROSSING PRESS

Psycho Kitty?: Understanding Your Cat's Crazy Behavior
By Pam Johnson-Bennett

Is your cat's behavior making you crazy? Johnson-Bennett believes that trying to understand how your cat thinks is a key to your cat's misbehavior. She shares real cases to illustrate various problems and explains how she arrives at an appropriate solution through behavior modification.
Paper • ISBN-13: 978-0-89594-909-7 / ISBN-10: 0-89594-909-1

Natural Healing for Dogs & Cats
By Diane Stein

Tells how to use nutrition, vitamins, minerals, massage, herbs, homeopathy, acupuncture, acupressure, and flower essences, as well as owner-pet communication and psychic healing.
Paper • ISBN-13: 978-0-89594-614-0 / ISBN-10: 0-89594-614-9

The Natural Remedy Book for Dogs & Cats
By Diane Stein

The perfect companion to Stein's earlier book- *Natural Healing for Dogs and Cats*. Fifty common pet ailments and remedies are arranged in alphabetical order. Methods of treatment including nutrition, naturopathy, vitamins and minerals, herbs, homeopathy, acupuncture/acupressure, flower essences, and gemstones are discussed for each illness.
Paper • ISBN-13: 978-0-89594-686-7 / ISBN-10: 0-89594-686-6

For a current catalog of books from The Crossing Press visit our Web site at: **www.tenspeed.com**.